HYMNS UNBIDDEN

HYMNS UNBIDDEN

Donne, Herbert, Blake, Emily Dickinson and the Hymnographers

By

MARTHA WINBURN ENGLAND

and

JOHN SPARROW

THE NEW YORK PUBLIC LIBRARY

Astor, Lenox and Tilden Foundations

1966

Library of Congress Catalog Card Number: 66–28617

© Copyright The New York Public Library 1966

Reprinted from the
Bulletin of The New York Public Library
April, December 1964, February 1965, January – April 1966
Printed at The New York Public Library
form p741 [ix-1-66 2m]

To Sir Geoffrey Keynes

Foreword

THE GENERAL SUBJECT of this group of studies is the hymn movement of the eighteenth century. Fathered by the Puritan hymnodist Isaac Watts, this movement is seen to have been nourished — more than anyone had realized — by transfusions from Herbert, Donne, and other metaphysical poets; to have been brought to immense power and range by the Wesleys; and to have exerted no simple influence upon the modes and tunes of subsequent English and American poets.

All this has until now remained knowledge hidden or remote to historians of "pure" literature, the hymn constituting an excluded category of literature "applied." Even to weekly singers of selected hymns, most of these matters must be unfamiliar, even unsuspected. Only perseverance and arcane bibliographic curiosity led Mr Sparrow to his discovery of poems shaped into hymns. Only the mastering of "Watts Entire" and "Wesley Entire" prepared Mrs England's sensitivity to parallels and resonances in the songs and epics of the nonecclesiastical William Blake and the antihymns of the solitary Puritan singer, Emily Dickinson.

To an editor's eye these studies offer the attractive prospect of new openings in the forest. Confirmatively, *Bulletin* readers have welcomed these efforts to widen the field and definition of literary history. For the neglect of hymnody as a genre and body of literature has kept the literary historian innocent of its values and ignorant of its relevance, unable to recognize its roots or its ramifications even in the work of his favorite poets. Mr Sparrow's discovery now establishes a continuity that seemed lacking. His and Professor England's investigations will appear at first entirely focussed on the hymn movement itself, with only a gleam of anticipation of its later influences. But we soon learn that the writers of hymns were themselves attentive to sources — that Watts and the Wesleys and John Gambold made record of their borrowings, and indeed that Gambold's hymn book was organized and arranged as an historical anthology of church song, the first of its kind.

The subsequent influences, outside hymnody proper, Mrs England pursues in the more familiar domains of Blake criticism and Emily Dickinson criticism. The soundness of her approach to the mysterious William Blake lies in the assumption that Blake was an ordinary man with ordinary and popular as well as literary sources. She sees the transmutation of Wesleyan hymns into Blakean epics partly as a process of creative digestion of the stuff of common life — with emphasis therefore not upon particular sources but upon the shared social, intellectual milieu of Wesley and Blake. (Some of her work in progress is the tracing of the "anthems" of Blake's satiric "Island in the Moon" through the media of stage pastoral and popular farce; at least she has some clues in the printed relics of such daily life.) That Blake read the Bible "day and night" we know, but we would like to be less ignorant of the complex of influences that caused him to "read black." The several exegetical scholars currently engaged in reading Blake's reading are herewith directed to attend to the hymns and oratory and mirth of his day, not so much for particular sources as for modes of reading all his bibles.

Another kind of assimilation by redirection, Emily Dickinson's association with the words and music of hymns, brings the tale around again to Watts. This leaves Watts and Wesley the unacknowledged legislators of more poetic law than either Dickinson or Blake can have felt comfortable with. The subject is thus enlarged and redefined but by no means closed.

DAVID V. ERDMAN

Contents

Illustrations

George Herbert and John Donne among the Moravians

THE ECLIPSE of Donne's poetry in the eighteenth century is a commonplace in the history of English literature. The original series of editions of his poems came to an end in 1669; Tonson published a duodecimo edition in 1719; after that, apart from the reprints included in the series of English Poets published by Bell (1779), Anderson (1793), and Chalmers (1810), no collected edition appeared until his nineteenth-century re-discoverers got to work. Pope and Parnell had "versified" three of his Satires in the 1730s, and Johnson had paraded a selection of his "metaphysical" monstrosities in his Life of Cowley (1779); but no other glimpse of Donne's poems was, it seems, afforded to readers of English poetry for a hundred years, and Sir Geoffrey Keynes's exhaustive Bibliography (3rd edition, 1958) contains only a score of references to him or to his works for the whole of the eighteenth century.

A similar eclipse befell other religious poets of the seventeenth century. Of Crashaw, nothing was printed after the original editions of the 1670s until a selection of his poetry, made by one Peregrine Phillips, appeared in 1785; he was included in Anderson's and Chalmers's collections, but no serious attention was paid to his poetry until the 1850s, in the course of which there appeared two (not very scholarly) editions of his Poetical Works. As for Vaughan, H. F. Lyte's edition of his *Sacred Poems* of 1847 was, according to Professor Martin (*The Works of Henry Vaughan*, Clarendon Press 1914 I xiv), "the first edition of a complete work of Henry Vaughan to be published since the seventeenth century."

About Herbert's reputation in the eighteenth century there is nearly the same tale to tell: there was no edition of *The Temple* between 1709 and 1799; "the standard collections of the English poets by Anderson, Chalmers and others," says Canon Hutchinson,[1] "generally ignore him," and "there are only a few individual writers and anthologists who keep him in remembrance." [2]

---

1 *The Works of George Herbert*, Clarendon Press 1941, p xlviii.

2 Ibid xlvi. An unusual admirer was the Rev John Wheeldon: see the Preface to his *Sacred Prolusions: or, Select Pieces from Bishop Taylor and Mr. Herbert*, 1768, where he quotes South's panegyric on Herbert: "Happy Genius! He was the better Man for being a Wit, and the best Way to praise him, is to quote him."

Of the "individual writers" who remembered Herbert, however, there was one who is outstanding: John Wesley. Canon Hutchinson, in the Introduction to his edition of Herbert's *Works*, called attention to Wesley's life-long admiration of *The Temple*, and in a separate article [3] he described how Wesley tried to spread the love of Herbert's poems among his followers. In 1744 Wesley introduced into his *Collection of Moral and Sacred Poems* (besides copious selections from Milton, Cowley, Norris, Congreve, Dryden, Addison, Prior, Pope, Parnell, Young and others) several poems from *The Temple*, abridging some of them but not otherwise altering the text; and in 1773, when he was seventy years old, he published *Select Parts of Mr. Herbert's Sacred Poems*, a collection of twenty-three poems from *The Temple* — abridgement, here again, being the only liberty with the text that he allowed himself to take.

Besides thus anthologizing Herbert's poems, Wesley proved his admiration of them by adapting them for congregational singing. Canon Hutchinson describes, in the article above referred to, how, when he crossed to America in 1735–6 in a ship that carried a company of Moravians, Wesley was impressed by the Brethren's addiction to hymn-singing. Soon after his arrival in Georgia, he began himself to compile a collection of hymns; and, having with him a copy of *The Temple*, he introduced into his collection, without any indication of their origin, adaptations of six of Herbert's poems, besides a number of the hymns of Isaac Watts. This collection was printed at Charlestown in 1737; [4] in the following year, after his return to England, he published in London an enlarged edition containing six more adaptations from Herbert. A year later appeared John and Charles Wesleys' *Hymns and Sacred Poems*; of the 138 pieces in this book, no fewer than forty-two were adaptations from Herbert (including ten of the twelve that he had already published); all were designated as being "From *Herbert*," and in almost every case they retained their original titles. [5]

"It is regrettable," says Canon Hutchinson, "that [Wesley] cut down Herbert's intricate metrical patterns to the Procrustean bed of Common, Long, and Short Measure, all of them iambic, to fit them for singing to familiar tunes." Wesley, he continues, pruned Herbert's conceits and gave his poems "an almost eighteenth century dress," but the adaptations, "however

---

[3] "John Wesley and George Herbert," *The London Quarterly*, August 1936.

[4] It is a rare volume; only two copies were known to Canon Hutchinson, writing in 1936. A facsimile, edited by Dr G. Osborn, was published by T. Woolmer (London, no date; the acquisition stamp in the Bodleian copy is dated 3 April 1883).

[5] There was, according to Hutchinson, a fourth edition, reduced in its content, from which about half the Herbert adaptations were omitted.

unsatisfactory, . . . made Herbert's poems known to an ever-widening circle of new readers in that age."

Wesley may have admired the Jacobean and Caroline religious poets generally — he must, it seems, have taken a copy of Donne's *Poems* with him to America, or else have known Donne's *Hymn to God the Father* well enough to quote it from memory, for he reproduced two lines from that hymn in his Journal while at sea on the return journey (24 January 1738) — but in his *Collection* he indulged his feeling for a single poet only, Herbert. His attempt thus to popularize Herbert with the Methodist congregations, however, cannot have had a lasting success, for when a canon of Methodist hymns was established in 1780 with the publication of *A Collection of Hymns for the use of the people called Methodists*, which has remained (with additions) the standard Methodist Hymnal, only one of Wesley's adaptations from the *The Temple* was retained.[6] Nor can I find in any of the Methodist collections adaptations from Donne, Crashaw, Vaughan or any other seventeenth-century poet.

On his return from America, Wesley continued for a time on good terms with the Moravians, but in 1740 he parted company with them, and we find him in his Journal for 15 December 1748 deriding the "nonsense and blasphemy" contained in "the last hymn-book published by Count Zinzendorf's Brethren." According to J. E. Hutton, the historian of the Movement, "nothing had brought greater ridicule upon the Brethren than the silly and indecent hymns they were supposed to sing," and in 1754, among other steps taken towards repelling hostile criticism, "they now issued, for the first time, an authorized official Moravian Hymn-Book." [7] As Hutton explains, "the Moravians were herein leading the way in a hitherto little-tried religious movement," for the Anglican Church at this time possessed no hymn-book, and the Moravian book "was of historic importance" and "exercised a permanent influence on the religious life of the nation." It was, Hutton continues, "a mirror of Moravian life. The chief burden of the hymns was the Passion History, every detail of which was commemorated in vivid realistic phrases. At times the language was almost gruesome, and the literary quality was decidedly poor. And yet . . . . with all their extravagances, the Moravian

---

6 This was *The Dialogue*, an adaptation of *Dialogue* (p 114 in Hutchinson's edition), with the omission of one stanza.

7 "The Moravian Contribution to the Evangelical Revival in England, 1742 to 1755," *Historical Essays by Members of the Owens College, Manchester* (Longmans 1902) 449. See also Hutton's *History of the Moravian Church*, 2nd ed 1909, p 362–364.

hymns contributed towards the diminution of the stern Calvinistic conception of Christianity associated with the Puritans, and the substitution of a
gentler, broader, and more human type of piety."

Neither the historians of the Moravian movement nor historians of the
literature or hymnology of the period seem to have appreciated one feature
of the hymn-book of 1754: it attempted to popularize, in the form of hymns
for congregational singing, a not inconsiderable body of the religious poetry
of the preceding century, including in particular a selection from the work
of the neglected poets (other than Henry Vaughan) mentioned above.

The first edition of the Moravian *Collection of Hymns* is a stout octavo of
more than 800 pages; [8] below (p 29) is a reproduction of its title-page.

The *Collection* was published at the instigation of Count Zinzendorf and
is said to have been printed at the private press which he installed for the
Brethren in Chelsea.[9] Zinzendorf was one of the most remarkable figures of
the eighteenth century in Europe; he was the "Ordinary" of the Unitas
Fratrum; he had revived the movement in Saxony, and he controlled it in
its extension in England. He was himself the author of a very large number
of the Brethren's German hymns, many of which were translated for the
Collection.[10] The editing of the *Collection* was delegated by Zinzendorf to
John Gambold,[11] one of the leaders of the English Moravian movement.[12]

---

[8] P [i]–[xii], prefatory matter; p 1–380, Part I; p 1–390, Part II; p [1]–[36] Tables, Index, etc.

[9] See *The Wesleyan Times*, 23 January 1865, p 58.

[10] A vivid portrait of Zinzendorf and a brilliant account of the Moravian movement are contained in Ch XVII of Mgr Ronald Knox's *Enthusiasm* (Oxford 1950 p 388–421).

[11] Benham, *Memoirs of James Hutton*, 1856, p 303. The following is the account given in the
official biography of Zinzendorf, by the Rev August Gottlieb Spangenberg (himself a Bishop
of the Moravian Church), published in eight parts, 1772–5 — I quote from the translation of
Samuel Jackson, 1838: "A commencement was also made this year [1753] in preparing an
English hymn-book, which appeared in 1754, under the title of 'A Collection of Hymns etc.'
Most of the hymns are translated from the German, and a variety of metres introduced, on
account of the melodies, which are not common in England. Besides these translations, the
hymn-book contains an excellent collection of hymns, originally English, of the sixteenth, seventeenth, and eighteenth centuries: there are also many select hymns translated from the Welsh
language."

[12] Gambold, who was born in 1711, went to Christ Church as a servitor, was ordained in 1733,
and in 1735 became Vicar of Stanton Harcourt in Oxfordshire; he left his parish in 1742 to
join the Moravians, and was consecrated a "Bishop" in 1754; he died in 1771. A brief Life of
Gambold is prefixed to the selection of his *Works* edited by La Trobe in 1789; Sir John Lloyd
contributed the article on him in the *DNB*; there is an appreciation of him, particularly as a
hymnologist, in an article in *The Wesleyan Times* 23 January 1865, p 58–59; and a whole
chapter is devoted to him in Tyerman's *The Oxford Methodists*, 1873. References to Gambold
will be found in Nichols' *Literary Anecdotes* (II 219–222) and throughout Benham's *Memoirs
of James Hutton*, which is a rich source for the history of the Moravian movement in England.

The *Collection* is divided into two Parts; the first Part comprises "Hymns of the Church in preceding Times," 695 in number; the second, "Hymns of the present Congregation of the Brethren," which number 460. The second Part is divided into two Sections, of which the first (which contains Hymns nos 1–302) covers the period from 1724 ("the time," according to Gambold's Preface, "from whence the present, or reviv'd Brethren's Congregation is to be dated") until 1744, and the second (which contains Hymns nos 303–460) the period from 1744 until 1754, the date when the *Collection* was published.

It is the second Part that contains the most characteristic Moravian hymns. Many of them — just one half of the 302 hymns in the first Section (1724–44), and just over two-thirds of the 158 hymns in the second (1744–54) — are translations from the German, taken in most cases (as the Editor explains in his Preface) from the Brethren's "*German* revis'd Hymn-book." [13] Some of them recount the annals of the Brethren, and illustrate Gambold's claim that the *Collection* provides "a Kind of Ecclesiastical History with regard to the state of Piety and Devotion":

> Thro' all the Centuries
> What Church-fruits fair and pleasant
> From one Blood-shedding rise,
> And from its pow'r incessant. . . .

> A Confessor could thus,
> 'Bout *Anno* fourteen hundred,
> Write sociably to *Huss*,
> Tho' the sky lowr'd and thunder'd. . .

> The Spirit does still remain
> Of Martydom, for instance,

[13] Presumably one of the revisions of the German Moravian Hymn-book, *Das Gesang-Buch der Gemeine in Herrnhut*, 1735. Gambold in a note to his Preface refers to Zinzendorf's contribution to the *Collection*, listing 35 Hymns in Part II as "his principal Hymns in this Book." These are translations from Zinzendorf's original German; he also contributed several hymns in English, including a versification of the Thirty-nine Articles, composed (according to Gambold) "out of respect for the Church of England."

The article in *The Wesleyan Times* above referred to declares, without revealing its authority, that Gambold contributed to the *Collection* 28 original hymns and some translations from the Greek, Latin or German. These "original" hymns are listed by the author of the article, but they are only 26 in number, and several are, in fact, translations from the German. Tyerman (*The Oxford Methodists*, p 192–193) repeats this without, apparently, observing the discrepancies. "Can these hymns be Gambold's?" he asks, continuing "We doubt it. Nay, we hope that they are not. It is scarcely possible to conceive, that a man of such culture could write such doggerel."

> No guilt suppos'd again
>   Of *Smithfield* or of *Constance*. . . .
>
> Note therefore, that since then,
>   This noblest ethick Method,
> Taught by Paul's Master-pen,
>   Has been to us bequeathed
> Afresh two hundred Year;
>   Since *Luther's* heart and mouth
> Kiss'd Jesu's Wounds, and there
>   Retriev'd the Chain of Truth.[14]

In others the note is doctrinal, or hortatory:

> One thing my heart engages
> In sweet Presages,
> That Jesus 'midst the Ages,
> Now gains a Flock!
> This Thought each smart asswages,
> Which else would shock:
> He'll lead thro' happy Stages,
> Tho' Satan rages,
> The Sinners who're his Wages;
> What safe Bank-stock! [15]

But the historical and doctrinal hymns, which are mostly to be found in the first Section (1724–44) of this Part, are not as striking as the Passion hymns that fill the second (1744–54) Section. "The Brethren's grand topic in their Hymns," says Gambold, "as every one may see, is the Person and Propitiation of *Jesus Christ*: they collect, as in the *Focus* of a Burning glass, what has descended to them from past Ages, or properly from the Bible itself, upon this Head." Every detail of the Passion History, as J. E. Hutton observes, was commemorated in "vivid realistic phrases" and in language that was at times "almost gruesome." It is not too much to say that among these hymns are some of the most remarkable literary (or, as Southey describes them, "illiterary") productions of the Age of Reason. The theme that inspired Toplady's impassioned prayer —

> Rock of Ages, cleft for me,
>   Let me hide myself in Thee! —

---

[14] Part II (Sect I) No 302 (original).
[15] Part II (Sect II) No 324 (original).

has an especial fascination for the Moravian hymnographers:

> Holy Side-wound, pierced *Pleura*,
>   Heart of Jesu, rent for me!
> Thou unfathomable Side-hole,
>   Fain would I be lost in thee.
>
> Ever a sure Rock-hole
> Art thou to my Man-Soul,
> Which from the Hole of the Pit
>   Hewn and split,
> Always weeps and pants for it.[16]

Sometimes this longing to find refuge in the "Pleura," the riven side of the Saviour, is (as it were) generalized, and the symbolic aspect of the sought-for union is prominent:

> Rejoice, ye hearts, in Jesu's Side!
>   Ye who're not in it, weep!
> The Side hole therefore is so wide,
>   So high, so broad, and deep,
> That all the Souls should enter there;
> Since therefore they created were,
> The Man with that sweet Rock-hole's space
> As Husband to embrace.
>
> The Church was like an Embryo,
>   Before her Husband dyed:
> But when the Side was pierced thro',
>   At once she was a Bride,
> Intitled to her Husband's Name,
> Out of whose Body forth she came;
> For she is truly Flesh and bone
> Of her Beloved one.[17]

At other times this same longing is expressed in more personal terms and in deeply passionate language:

> I cannot possibly leave off!
> I have not thee embrac'd enough;
> I kiss thee yet once more
> On thy bespittled bloody Cheeks;
> My longing must have what it seeks
> On thy unnumber'd Wounds and Sores.

[16] Part II (Sect II) No 447 (tr from German).
[17] Part II (Sect II) No 319 (original).

Upon thy Head I kiss the prints
Made by the num'rous thorny Points,
I kiss the Feet and Hands,
The Back depriv'd of skin and flesh,
The Cov'nant Blood's so early gash,
The Cave which in thy pierc'd Side stands.[18]

Sometimes the intensity of his feeling excites the worshipper almost to the point of incoherence:

To th' Side looking constantly,
So *Pleura* homesick inwardly,
His Heart to creep thro' so intent,
So smelling for his Blood-sweat's scent
On the magnetic Side;
So like a drop of Jesu's Sweat;
So quivering with Love's ague sweet,
Like th' inspired Infant;
So drawing breath in Corpse's Air,
So spouting forth Wound's Odour clear,
So from Grave's Vapours in a dew,
So panting the Son's sign to view. . . .[19]

Nor, in the vehemence of his devotion, does the Moravian enthusiast shrink from images that are positively gruesome —

Yes, Corpse like dewy now,
   And still grave-steaming Fingers!
Your Servant's bone sweat thro',
   Which quiv'ring for it lingers.
Thou Corpse's Air! come, come
   Thro' these hands into th'Bread:
When kneaded with thy Fume,
   'Twill make the Members dead.[20]

or language that is outrageously grotesque:

Thou Reason's Labyrinth,
   Thou *Tohu Vehabohu*
For the confed'rate troop
   Of Blood-Light-shunning *Uhu*;

[18] Part II (Sect II) No 432 (tr from German).
[19] Part II (Sect II) No 439 (original).
[20] Part II (Sect II) No 350 (tr from German).

> We Sinners, who surround
> Thy Side's dear cavity,
> Agree that in this Wound
> We'll dwell eternally.[21]

Even more remarkable are the hymns that introduce the "Cross-air birds" — doves, which the worshipper, endowing his devotional aspirations with living wings, imagines swarming about the Saviour's crucified body:

> What does a dove in Cross's Air,
> When enter-in it will and dare?
> The Cross's Breezes fill the sail
> And blow the bird to the Corpse pale.
> The wings hang faintly down,
> The dove would drop down soon,
> Had not its little Bill peck'd in
> Quite fast between the flesh and skin
> Of the Lamb's Body.
> There, as on Magnet, hangs the bird;
> It hangs, not choosing to be stirr'd;
> It lets all Time run on its pace,
> Cares nought for all Eternities,
> Saith "Be in glory living,
> Ye saints, let me be cleaving!"
>
> But what does the dear Bride-groom-Heart
> To such a Love with his Love's art,
> Whom he on Earth would wake and move,
> 'Cause it sha'n't yet fly up above?
> That does the Husband true
> In this sweet manner do;
> As he beholds the loyal Dove
> By his Side-shrine asleep for love,
> Which in had bitten,
> Upon the eye that fell asleep,
> And on the bill peck'd in so deep,
> At once a Blood-stream he does pour,
> Which flows the little bird all o'er;
> Thus loos'd, the bird must venture
> Its Flight afresh to enter.[22]

---

[21] Part II (Sect II) No 406 (tr from German). *Tohu Vehabohu* is explained in a note as "Chaos, without form and void"; *Uhu*, as "Owls."

[22] Part II (Sect II) No 355 (tr from German). Andrew Frey, in his *True and Authentic Account of the Moravians*, (see the quotations in Bishop Lavington's *The Moravians Compared and Detected*, 1755) gives some incredible parallels to the "cross-air birds," too blasphemous to be quoted here.

The identification of the "Cross-air bird" with the worshipper himself is made explicit in no 460, perhaps the most remarkable — it is also last in order — of the hymns in Part II (Section II) of the Collection:

We greet each other in the Side
    Of our beloved Spouse,
Which is ordain'd for his dear Bride
    Her everlasting House.
The Lamb, the Husband of our hearts,
Hath got, 'tis true, more wounded Parts,
Yet is the bleeding lovely Side
The Chamber of the Bride.

Our Husband's Side-wound is indeed
    The Queen of all his Wounds;
On this the little Pidgeons feed,
    Whom Cross's Air surrounds.
There they fly in and out and sing,
Side's Blood is seen on ev'ry wing,
The bill that picks the Side-hole's floor
Is red of Blood all o'er.

There sings the little happy crowd,
    Warbling their blood wash'd throats,
No other Bird however proud
    Can imitate their Notes.
They sing their *Pleurae gloria*!
And to the Lamb *Victoria*!
Amen and Amen sings the choir,
Then flies in to respire.

Blest flock in th'Cross's Atmosphere,
    You smell of Jesu's Grave,
The Vapours of his Corpse so dear
    Are the Perfume you have.
It's Scent is penetrant and sweet!
When you each other kiss and greet,
This Scent discovers that you were
To Jesu's Body near.

With thy Side's Blood quite cover me,
    And wet me thro' and thro';
For this I pant incessantly,
    And nothing else will do.
The Blood sweat in thy Agony
Come in full heat all over me,

> Thy Body stretch its breadth and length
> O'er me, and give me Strength.
>
> A bird that dives into the Side,
>   Goes down quite to the Ground,
> And finds a Bottom large and wide
>   In this so lovely Wound.
> A Side-hole's diver will I be.
> O Side-hole! I will sink in thee.
> My Soul and Body, enter thou
> Into the *Pleura* now.[23]

Half a century later Southey, in his Life of Wesley, passed judgement on the hymnody of the Moravians: "Even in the humours and the extravagances of the Spanish religious poets," he wrote, "there is nothing which approaches to the monstrous perversion of religious feeling in these astonishing productions," [24] and it is not surprising that the publication of hymns like these in England in the middle of the eighteenth century should have brought contempt and ridicule upon the Moravian movement.[25]

Many of the hymns contained in Part II of the *Collection* of 1754 had already been published in a *Collection* which appeared in three successive Parts during the 1740s,[26] and it was the third of these Parts that provoked Wesley's scornful exclamation, already quoted, about the nonsense and blasphemy contained in the hymns of Count Zinzendorf's Brethren; and in the same entry in his Journal for December 1748 he goes on to say that he has transcribed what he sarcastically calls "a few of these wonderful hymns" as a standing proof of "Moravian folly." Not only did Wesley transcribe a score of hymns from the third Part of A *Collection of Hymns* (1748), but he actually had them printed and published, anonymously, in 1749 with the satirical title *Hymns Composed for the Use of the Brethren By the Right*

---

[23] Part II (Sect II) No 460 (original).

[24] *Life of Wesley*, Ch V note XX.

[25] The Brethren did their best to remedy this situation by bringing out in 1778 a new hymnbook, edited by Christian Gregor, which was "absolutely free from extravagant language" (see Hutton, *History of the Moravian Church*, 1909, p 415–416).

[26] A *Collection of Hymns with several translations from the Hymn Book of the Moravian Brethren*: Part I, 1742 (2nd ed 1743; 3rd ed 1746); Part II, 1746; Part III, 1748 (2nd ed 1749). The hymns in the first edition of Part I are numbered 1–187, to which the second edition adds nos 188–239; those in Part II, 240–403; those in the first edition of Part III, 1–126, to which the second edition adds 127–161.

Reverend, and most Illustrious C. Z. Published for the Benefit of all Mankind.[27]

Wesley's ironical preface is worth quoting in full:

To the Reader

The following Hymns are copied from a Collection printed some months since, for *James Hutton* in *Fetter-lane, London.* You will easily observe, That they have no Affinity at all to that old Book called *The Bible*: The Illustrious Author soaring as far above this, as above the beggarly Elements of *Reason* and *Commonsense.*

It was as a counter to attacks of this sort, according to Hutton, that Gambold, at Zinzendorf's direction, published for the Brethren the official Hymnal of 1754. One might have supposed that Gambold would have purged the Moravian corpus of hymns like those quoted above, and in particular that he would have omitted specimens that had been held up to ridicule by Wesley; but this was not the case. The *Collection* of 1754 retains about half of the hymns that had appeared in the three Parts of the earlier collection,[28] and includes, among them, the same proportion (ten out of twenty) of the hymns reprinted in Wesley's mocking pamphlet;[29] in many of the hymns the text is altered, in varying degrees; but neither omissions

---

[27] A more celebrated effort in ridicule of the Brethren was Anstey's in *The New Bath Guide*, 1766, where

> . . . Tabby from Scruples of Mind is releas'd,
> Since she met with a learned Moravian Priest,
> Who says, *There is neither Transgression nor Sin*;
> A Doctrine that brings many Customers in.

Anstey also gives an example of Moravian hymnody, which he says "the learned Moravian pirated . . . . . from Count Zinzendorf's Book of Hymns":

> Chicken blessed
> And caressed,
> Little Bee on Jesu's Breast.

This is taken from No 412 in the Second Part of the *Collection* of 1754, a hymn of ten lines, which begins and ends as follows:

> Infant blessed and caressed,
> Little Bee on Jesu's Breast . . .
> Chicken blessed, bee caressed,
> Thou that sleep'st on Jesu's Breast.

[28] At least, it repeats about half the contents of Part I (1742) and of Part III (1748); I have not had access to a copy of Part II (1746).

[29] The following are the numbers of the hymns in Part III (1748) so reprinted by Wesley, followed, in the case of each hymn reprinted in Part II of the *Collection* of 1754, by the number (bracketed) that it bears in that collection: 24 (394), 33, 42, 43, 46, (346), 51, 57, 59, 61 (438), 64, 71 (406), 75 (344), 76, 83, 89, 95 (392), 97 (288), 100 (376), 106 (418), 111 (355). Wesley allows himself some liberties with the texts, and in some cases prints only selected stanzas of a hymn.

nor alterations, it is plain, were dictated by a desire to prune or mitigate such extravagances as had provoked Wesley's scorn.[30]

Gambold chose a different method of rendering the Moravian hymnology respectable: he decided to incorporate the "Hymns of the present Congregation of the Brethren" in a collection containing over a thousand hymns, so that they should take their place in a historical sequence in which they were preceded by specimens of the hymnody of the Church in all the ages. Gambold was well fitted for this undertaking; he had been distinguished in classical studies as an undergraduate at Christ Church, and he was a student of early Church history, and of the Fathers. "He was at a certain time so given up, if we may thus express it," says La Trobe, "to the company of the fathers, and so taken with their manners, that he unintentionally became in his way of thinking, speaking, and acting, as though he had lived in the first or second century, and in the closest intimacy with Ignatius, Polycarp, &c." His *Collection* of 1754 provides a remarkable conspectus of hymnology from the days of the primitive Church, through the period of the first Moravians and the German Reformation, down to the century immediately preceding his own. Part I of the *Collection*, "Hymns of the Church in preceding Times," is a retrospective anthology, divided into nine Sections, the titles of which (with the numbers of the hymns contained in each of them) are as follows:

1. Anthems out of the Bible (nos 1–110)
2. Scripture Hymns (nos 111–181)
3. Hymns of the Primitive Church (nos 182–245)
4. Hymns of the ancient Brethren (nos 246–297)
5. *German* Hymns in the xvi[th] Century (nos 298–336)
6. Old Hymns of the *English* Church (nos 337–431)
7. *German* Hymns in the xvii[th] Century (nos 432–481)
8. *English* Hymns of the same Age (nos 482–536)
9. Hymns, *German* and *English*, about the End of the xvii[th], or in the xviii[th] Century (nos 537–695)

In his Preface Gambold describes the contents of these Sections. The first, he says, contains "*Anthems out of the Bible*; sacred Words, that are and must be laid as the Foundation of all"; the second, "*Scripture-Hymns*; or

---

[30] Dr Louis Benson, in the full and otherwise accurate account of the *Collection* in his *The English Hymn, Its Development and Use in Worship* (1915) p 264–269, says that "only two of the hymns selected by Wesley were reprinted in the 1754 book" — a statement which is accurate only if interpreted as meaning "reprinted verbatim." Dr Benson gives an excellent account of Moravian hymnography; but he failed to observe the origin of the "Old Hymns of the English Church" discussed in this article. See also note on p 28.

Portions of Scripture put into Metre either already by others, or now by us." The Hymns in the third Section, which covers the whole period of the Fathers, "are not many, considering what an Interval they fill up; but they are weighty, and taken from all the chief Branches of the Church universal" (they include translations of *Veni, Creator, Jesu dulcis memoria,* and *Pange lingua*); in the fourth Section are hymns of "the ancient *Bohemian and Moravian Brethren.* (The *Waldenses* incorporated with them)." There follow in the fifth Section, says Gambold, "*German Hymns* . . . made about the Time of the Reformation," and he acknowledges, "in regard of the Translation," the "considerable Use we have made (here and in some other Parts) of the foregoing labours of Mr. *Jacobi,* and the Rev. Mr. Wesley."

Passing over for the moment the sixth Section, we come, in the seventh and eighth, to German and English hymns, respectively, "of the *seventeenth Century.*" As we shall see, the sixth Section consists of English pieces belonging mostly to the early and middle years of the seventeenth century; those in the eighth Section belong mostly to its latter part — "The Authors," says the editor, "are Bishop *Kenn,* Mr. *Norris,* Rawlet, Mason, &c." — and some (e.g. no 531, Watts's "When all thy Mercies, O my God") belong to the eighteenth century. The English hymns in the ninth Section are likewise drawn from both the seventeenth and the eighteenth centuries, though most of them are "of the *Eighteenth,* or now current Century, which indeed" (says the editor) "has been the richest in that kind of writing that *England* can ever remember. The Names here," he continues, "are very recent and well known, as Dr. *Watts, Stennet, Davis, Erskine, Wesley, Cennick,* &c."

The hymns in the seventh, eighth and ninth Sections of Part I carry no signatures,[31] and the only indications of their authorship are the references, just quoted, in Gambold's Preface; where a hymn is translated from the German, however, the opening words of the original are printed at the head of the translation.

The sixth Section, containing "Old Hymns of the *English* Church," is especially interesting. In this Section some clues are given in the text to the source or authorship of the contents (nos 337–431). The first twelve of these ninety-five pieces are not marked or signed in any way; their source is indicated at the end of the twelfth piece (no 348), by the words "*Hactenus è Liturgiâ Eccl. Angl.*"; the thirteenth (no 349, a piece only eight lines long) is headed "A Parody upon that old Verse, *Whoso him bethoft.*" Of the

---

[31] Save that no 676, a second version of *Pange lingua,* misplaced in this Section, is attributed to "Fortunat. Ep."

remaining eighty-two pieces (nos 350–431) ten (and ten only) carry the distinctive mark "†" printed against the number of the hymn. Of the ten marked pieces, seven are signed, six (nos 353, 383, 385, 393, 403, 411) with one or more initials, one (no 431) with a name; three (nos 415, 422, 427) are unsigned. Only one hymn (no 350) not marked with a † is signed. The following list shows the arrangement:

350	signed	"R.S."	351–352	unsigned
353 †	"	"H."	354–382	"
383 †	"	"D."	384	"
385 †	"	"F.T."	386–392 [32]	"
393 †	"	"C."	394–402	"
403 †	"	"T."	404–410	"
411 †	"	"M.H."	412–414	"
415 † unsigned [33]			416–421	" [33]
422 †	"		423–426	"
427 †	"		428–430	"
431 † signed *"Masters."*				

The significance of these marks and signatures appears from what the editor says in his Preface about the sixth Section:

> Then come (and I mention it with a peculiar Pleasure) some excellent *old Hymns of the English Church.* The Authors, besides the *Common-prayer Book* itself, are *Robert Smith, Herbert,* Dr. *Donne, Faithful Teate, Crashaw,* Bishop *Taylor,* Sir *Matthew Hale, Rees Pritchard* the *Welch* Hymnologist, &c. Some of these, particularly *Herbert,* having wrote in Stanza's adapted to no Tune that we know of, a Liberty has been taken sometimes so far as to make them singable, yet with as little Alteration as possible of the Sense.

With this key to the text, it is easy to see that a " † " marks the start of a series of hymns by a new author, and one can make the following attributions:

---

[32] Among the "Notanda" on the last page of the *Collection* is the following: "When Hymns have, through Oversight, been placed out of their due Class and Age, it has usually been remark'd; whereto add Part I. No 660 (which ought to have follow'd next after 392)." From this it appears that no 660 (which consists of 27 stanzas; its first line is "Rose! without prickles of thy own") belongs to the "F T" series.

[33] Nos 415–421 are translations from the Welsh, the opening words of the original being in each case printed at the head of the hymn.

350–2	Robert Smith	411–414	Sir Matthew Hale
353–382	George Herbert	415–421	Rees Prichard
383–4	John Donne	422–426	?
385–392 [34]	Faithful Teate	427–430	?
393–402	Richard Crashaw	431	Thomas Masters
403–410	Jeremy Taylor		

HERBERT   The principal contributor, it will be seen, was Herbert, no fewer than thirty of whose poems appear in adaptation (including four from Harvey's *Synagogue*, which was regularly bound up with later editions of *The Temple*). One naturally suspects that these are borrowed from the group of adaptations of Herbert published in Wesley's *Hymns and Sacred Poems* of 1739. A glance at the Appendix A, however, will show that this is not so; of the thirty adaptations in the Moravian collection (nos 353–382) only ten are versions of poems already adapted by Wesley, and in six of these ten cases Gambold's differs entirely from Wesley's version; in four cases only his text reproduces Wesley's (sometimes with abridgements) identically or with little variation.[35]

Two specimens will indicate the sort of relationship that Wesley's and Gambold's versions bear to each other and to their original in Herbert.[36]

HERBERT	WESLEY	MORAVIAN COLLECTION
The Dawning	*The Dawning.*	Part I, no 360
	From Herbert	
		Easter

HERBERT — *The Dawning*

Awake sad heart, whom sorrow ever drowns;
Take up thine eyes, which
feed on earth;
Unfold thy forehead gath-
er'd into frowns:
Thy Saviour comes, and
with him mirth:
Awake, awake;
And with a thankfull heart
his comforts take.
But thou dost still lament,
and pine, and crie;
And feel his death, but not
his victorie.

WESLEY — *The Dawning.* From Herbert

I

Awake, sad Heart, whom
Sorrows drown,
Lift up thine Eyes, and
cease to mourn,
Unfold thy Forehead's
settled Frown;
Thy Saviour, and thy Joys
return.

II

Awake, sad drooping Heart,
awake!
No more lament, and
pine, and cry:
His Death Thou ever dost
partake,
Partake at last his Victory.

MORAVIAN COLLECTION — Part I, no 360 — *Easter*

1. Awake, sad Heart, whom
sorrow drowns!
Unfold thy forehead from
its frowns,
Take up thine eyes which
feed on earth,
Thy Saviour comes, and
with him mirth!
He left his Grave-cloaths,
that we might, when
grief
Draws sighs and tears, not
want a Handkerchief.

[34] To these (see note 31 above) should be added no 660.

[35] Gambold did not avail himself of thirty-two of Wesley's forty-two adaptations, and chose to adapt twenty poems not chosen by Wesley for adaptation.

[36] Gambold's text diverges rather more than usually from Herbert's in the specimens chosen.

HERBERT

Arise sad heart; if thou doe
   not withstand,
   Christs resurrection thine
      may be:
Do not by hanging down
   break from the hand,
   Which as it riseth, raiseth
   thee:
              Arise, arise;
And with his buriall-linen
   drie thine eyes:
   Christ left his grave-
   clothes
      that we might, when
      grief
Draws tears, or blood, not
   want a handkerchief.

WESLEY

III

Arise; if thou dost not with-
   stand,
   Christ's Resurrection
   Thine may be:
O break not from the
   Gracious Hand
   Which, as it rises, raises
   Thee.

IV

Chear'd by thy Saviour's
   Sorrows rise;
He griev'd, That Thou
   mayst cease to grieve;
Dry with his Burial Clothes
   thine Eyes,
He dy'd Himself, that
   Thou mayst live!

MORAVIAN COLLECTION

2. Now, heart! if thou dost
   not withstand,
Nor, hanging down, break
   from his Hand,
Christ's Resurrection thine
   may be;
He, as he riseth, raiseth
   thee,
That as his Death had cal-
   cin'd thee to dust,
His Life may make thee
   Gold, and much more
   just.

HERBERT

Ephes. 4. 30
Grieve not the Holy Spirit, &c

And art thou grieved, sweet
   and sacred Dove,
When I am soure,
   And crosse thy love?
Grieved for me? the God of
   strength and power
Griev'd for a worm, which
   when I tread,
   I passe away and leave it
   dead?

Then weep mine eyes, the
   God of love doth
   grieve:
      Weep foolish heart,
      And weeping live:
For death is drie as dust.
      Yet if ye part,
End as the night, whose
   sable hue
Your sinnes expresse; melt
   into dew.

What sawcie mirth shall
      knock or call at doore,
      Cry out, Get hence,
      Or cry no more.
Almightie God doth grieve,
   he puts on sense:
I sinne not to my grief alone,
But to my Gods too; he doth
   grone.

WESLEY

Grieve not the Holy Spirit.
From the same [sc. Herbert]

I

And art thou griev'd, O
   Sacred Dove,
When I despise or cross thy
   Love?
Griev'd for a Worm; when
   ev'ry Tread
Crushes, and leaves the
   Reptile dead!

III

Then weep, my Eyes, for
   GOD doth grieve!
Weep, foolish Heart, and
   weeping live:
Tears for the Living
   Mourner plead,
But ne'er avail the hopeless
   Dead.

II

Then Mirth be ever banish'd
   hence,
Since Thou art pain'd by my
   Offence;
I sin not to my Grief alone,
The Comforter within doth
   groan.

MORAVIAN COLLECTION

Part I no 368

1. And art thou griev'd,
   sweet sacred Dove,
When I am sour, and cross
   thy love?
Griev'd for a worm, which
   when I tread,
I pass away and leave it
   dead?

2. I sin not to my grief
   alone,
But to my God's too; he
   doth groan.
Weep, eyes! the God of love
   doth grieve
Weep, foolish heart! and
   weeping live.

HERBERT	WESLEY	MORAVIAN COLLECTION

Oh take thy lute, and tune it to a strain,
    Which may with thee
    All day complain.
There can no discord but inceasing be.
    Marbles can weep; and surely strings
More bowels have, then such hard things.		

Lord, I adjudge myself to tears and grief,
    Ev'n endlesse tears
    Without relief.
If a cleare spring for me no time forbears,
    But runnes, allthough I be not drie;
    I am no Crystall, what shall I?
	IV
	Lord, I adjudge myself to Grief,
	To endless Tears without Relief:
	Yet O! t'exact thy Due forbear,
	And spare a feeble Creature, spare!	

Yet if I wail not still, since still to wail
        Nature denies;
        And flesh would fail,
If my deserts were masters of mine eyes:
        Lord, pardon, for thy Sonne makes good
    My want of tears with store of blood.
	V
	Still if I wail not, (still to wail
	Nature denies, and Flesh would fail)
	Lord, pardon — for thy Son makes good
	My Want of Tears, with Store of Blood.
		3. Still if I wail not (still to wail,
		Nature denies, and flesh would fail)
		Lord, pardon! for the Son mades good
		My want of tears with Store of Blood.

CRASHAW   After Herbert, the poet from whom Gambold takes most is Crashaw, of whom there are ten adaptations (nos 393–402). Particulars of these are given in Appendix B. The adapter allows himself to select and abridge, but he does not alter the text much more than is necessary in order to make it fit existing tunes, e.g.:

> Whatever story of their cruelitie
> Or Naile, or Thorne, or Spears have writ in Thee,
>   Are in another sence
>   Still legible;
> Sweet is the difference:
>   Once I did spell
> Every red letter
>   A wound of thine,
> Now, (what is better)
>   Balsome for mine.
>
> (Crashaw: *On the still surviving markes of our Saviours wounds*)

What stories of their cruelty
Nail, Thorn or Spear have writ in thee,
Are in two ways still legible:
I once did understand and spell
Ev'ry red Letter as a Wound of thine,
Now, which is better, as a Balm for mine.

(*M Collection* Part I no 396)

DONNE   The most interesting, and perhaps the most surprising, of the adaptations contained in Part I of the Moravian *Collection* are those numbered 383 and 384. The first of these consists of fourteen stanzas of four decasyllabic lines, which comprise four of Donne's *Holy Sonnets* dovetailed together; the second consists of the first three (9-line) stanzas of Donne's *The Litanie*, abridged into six stanzas of four lines each; see Appendix C.

The four sonnets chosen to compose Hymn no 383 are nos I (Thou hast made me, and shall thy worke decay), II (As due by many titles I resigne), XI (Spit in my face you Iewes, and pierce my side), and XIII (What if this present were the world's last night?). The lines being decasyllabic, no metrical alteration within the line was necessary, and the adapter made no change in the octave of any of the four sonnets; but the last six lines in each case created difficulties which he overcame by a good deal of reshuffling.

In Sonnet I, the first four lines of the sestet are left unaltered, and the concluding couplet provides the first and fourth lines of the Hymn's fourth stanza, the second and third lines of which are fetched from the concluding couplet of Sonnet II, thus:

<table>
<tr><td align="center">DONNE</td><td align="center">MORAVIAN COLLECTION</td></tr>
<tr><td align="center">*Holy Sonnet* I lines 13, 14</td><td align="center">Part I no 383 st 4</td></tr>
<tr><td>Thy Grace may wing me to prevent his art
And thou like adamant draw mine iron heart.</td><td>Do thou, like adamant, draw mine iron Heart:
Lo, Satan hates me, yet is loth to lose me;
Thou lovest mankind well, yet wilt not choose me!</td></tr>
<tr><td align="center">*Holy Sonnet* II lines 12–14</td><td>So he suggests; do thou prevent his Art.</td></tr>
<tr><td>Oh I shall soone despaire, when I shall see
That thou lov'st mankinde well, yet wilt not chuse me,
And Satan hates me, yet is loath to lose me.</td><td></td></tr>
</table>

Sonnet II, having thus lost its concluding couplet, provides, with its first twelve lines, the next three stanzas (5–7) of the Hymn, the twelfth line being altered to "Oh! I shall soon despair, and conquer'd be" in order to end with the end of the stanza.

Sonnet XI provides, with its octave, the next two stanzas (8, 9) of the hymn, and lines 9–12 of the sonnet make up stanza 10, without alteration, save that lines 11 and 12 are transposed (and slightly reworded) — presumably in order to preserve the *abba* rhyme-scheme (which was, however, abandoned in the third and sixth stanzas of the hymn). The concluding couplet provides, without alteration, the second and third lines of the next (eleventh) stanza, the first and fourth being manufactured by the adapter, thus:

> But my celestial Lord had other views;
> God cloth'd himself in vile man's Flesh, that so
> He might be weak enough to suffer Woe.
> Canst thou yet dread, when thou on this dost muse?

Finally, Sonnet XIII provides, with its octave, the twelfth and thirteenth stanzas, and the fourteenth consists of its sestet with two (clearly unsuitable) lines omitted and the rest re-shuffled, thus:

DONNE	MORAVIAN COLLECTION
Holy Sonnet XIII, lines 9–14	Part I no 383 st 14
No, no; but as in my idolatrie	To wicked spirits are horrid shapes assign'd;
I said to all my profane mistresses,	Beauty's of Pity, foulness only is
Beauty, of pitie, foulnesse only is	A Sign of rigour: th'inference then is wise,
A signe of rigour: so I say to thee,	*This* beauteous Form assures a piteous Mind.
To wicked spirits are horrid shapes assigned,	
This beauteous forme assures a piteous minde.	

No 384 in the Moravian *Collection* consists of the first three stanzas of Donne's *The Litanie*; the adapter has made only such alterations as were necessary in order to turn each of Donne's three nine-line stanzas into two stanzas each of four lines.

FAITHFULL TEATE   The next eight hymns (nos 385–392) are taken, as in no 660, from Faithfull Teate's *Ter Tria: Or the Doctrine of the Three Sacred Persons, Father, Son, and Spirit*, 1658. Gambold picks and chooses his material from the hundreds of rambling stanzas of which Teate's *Father, Son, Spirit, Hope,* and *Love,* are composed: nos 385 and 386 (containing ten and three stanzas respectively) are from *Father*; nos 387–389 (four lines, six stanzas and seven stanzas respectively) are from *Son*; no 390 (twelve stanzas) is from *Spirit*; no 391 (five stanzas) is from *Hope*; and no 392 (seven stanzas) and no 660 (27 stanzas) are from *Love*. Appendix D indicates the extent to which Gambold has adapted his original in each case.

JEREMY TAYLOR   Eight hymns (nos 403–410) are taken from "Festival Hymns, According to the manner of *The Ancient Church*," a score or so of poems appended to Jeremy Taylor's *The Golden Grove* (1655). The text is evidently taken from a later edition. In almost every case the adaptations are extremely free, as will appear from Appendix E.

SIR MATTHEW HALE   The Jeremy Taylor hymns are followed by adaptations (nos 411–414) of four of the seventeen "Poems upon Christmas Day," printed at the end of Part I of Sir Matthew Hale's *Contemplations Moral and Divine* (1676). The text is evidently taken from the 1679, or a later edition. Appendix F indicates how far the originals have been adapted.

RHYS PRICHARD   The seven hymns (nos 415–421) which form the next group are translations of hymns composed in Welsh by Rhys Prichard. Prichard, who was Vicar of Llandovery from 1602 until his death in 1644, was famous throughout the Principality for his versified sermons, written in colloquial Welsh. "So popular was he as a preacher," says Sir John Lloyd in his account of Prichard in the *DNB*, "that on many occasions he was forced to speak in the open air," and though his verses were not printed in his lifetime, three series of them appeared successively in the decades succeeding his death, and in 1672 a comprehensive collection of them was issued by Stephen Hughes, a non-conformist preacher, under the title *Canwyll y Cymry* ("The Welshman's Candle"). "Vicar Prichard's" verses maintained their popularity in Wales throughout the eighteenth century: editions were published at Shrewsbury in 1714, 1721, 1725, 1740 and 1766, and in 1770 there appeared an entirely new and revised edition, with the alternative title *Y Seren Foreu* ("The Morning Star") and a large number of additional poems from what were believed to be the author's mss; this was itself reprinted at Carmarthen in 1776, 1798, and 1808. The definitive edition appeared at Llandovery in 1841 (reprinted, 1858, 1867); this was the (posthumously published) work of Price Rees of Lampeter, who provided explanatory notes and a full biography.

All the editions mentioned above reproduced the Welsh text of Prichard's verses: it was not until 1771 that a complete English translation was offered to the public.[37] The translator, William Evans, Vicar of Lanhaden, declared

---

[37] *The Welshman's Candle: or the Divine Poems of Mr. Rees Prichard. . . . Now first translated into English Verse*, Carmarthen 1771. This was reprinted, under the title *The Morning Star, or, the Divine Poems of Mr. Rees Prichard*, at Merthyr Tydfil in 1815.

in his Preface that "the Translator assumes no more Merit to himself from this Performance than that it is the only Translation of Mr Prichard's Poems, hitherto publish'd." [38]

Fifty years later one John Bulmer published a version of Prichard's poems [39] which might, he said in his Preface, "be regarded as an improvement of Mr Evans's Version, intended not so much for the Welsh, to whom the poems are already known, as for the English, to whom they are unknown." Evans's translation, says Bulmer, "was the only translation ever offered to the public. It was printed" (he continues) "by subscription at Carmarthen, and not being sold any where in England, must have been entirely unknown beyond the principality, except to a few of the Translator's friends."

Both Evans's and Bulmer's versions of those poems of Prichard that are included in the Moravian *Collection* differ so completely from the versions there given by Gambold that it is clear that they made no use of Gambold's translations, and the translators were no doubt perfectly sincere in their claim that Evans's was the first translation of Prichard ever published — an assertion that, so far as I know, has remained unchallenged until today.[40]

There seems to be no reason to doubt that Gambold himself was responsible for the translations of Prichard in the Moravian Collection,[41] and it is presumably these translations that explain the statement in the article in

---

[38] He had thought (he confesses) of abridging the poems (which, in his translation, fill 480 large octavo pages), but "thought himself obliged to drop that Design, as soon as he considered that the far greater Part of the *Welsh* would have deem'd it a high Piece of Presumption, at least, in him, if not a Sacrilege, to have either alter'd or diminish'd any Part of their beloved Author's Work."

[39] *The Vicar of Llandovery, or Light from the Welshman's Candle*, Haverfordwest, 1821. A second edition was published in London in 1830 under the title *Beauties of the Vicar of Llandovery*. Bulmer considerably abridged the text and rewrote what he retained; he re-arranged the poems, and provided copious annotations; his version differs so radically from Evans's that it must be considered to be a new translation.

[40] The Rev T. J. Morris, of Pentrefelin Vicarage, Criccieth, has called my attention, however, to the fact that in *Y Per Ganiedydd-Pantycelyn* (Aberystwyth 1958 p 12) G. M. Roberts observes that Gambold did not "see fit to translate any Welsh material for his 'Hymns for the Children of God in all ages' 1754, *other than a few of the Vicar Prichard's verses* [my italics]." This observation (kindly translated for me from the Welsh by Mr Morris) and the remarks in *The Wesleyan Times* must be taken as qualifying the words in my text to which this note is appended.

[41] He was himself a Pembrokeshire man, and during his last years at Haverfordwest, according to his biographer, La Trobe, he "drew up some remarks on the Welsh tongue, and grammatical institutions in that language, for the use of English preachers." According to the article on the Gambold family in *The Dictionary of Welsh Biography* (published "under the Auspices of the Honourable Society of Cymmrodorion" in 1959), Gambold published in 1770 a Welsh Moravian hymn-book, containing three hymns from Prichard and 34 versions by Gambold himself of English Moravian hymns; of which "it must be confessed," says R. T. Jenkins, the author of the article, "that they are rather stiff."

The Wesleyan Times already referred to (quoted by Gordon in his account of Gambold in the *DNB*) that Gambold "was the first to translate the 'Divine Poems' of Rees Prichard from Welsh into English." At all events, it is plain that the Moravian *Collection* of 1754 precedes by nearly twenty years what has hitherto been supposed to be the first translation of Prichard's verses and that, if Bulmer is right in saying that Evans's translation was "not . . . sold anywhere in England," it provided the only specimen of his hymnody available to English congregations in the eighteenth century.

ROBERT SMITH   The author of nos 350–352 must, I think, be Robert Smith, "School-Master at Glammis, Forfarshire," whose *Metrical Version of the Assembly's Shorter Catechism* (Edinburgh 1729; a little book of extreme rarity already in 1872, when a reprint of 70 copies was issued in Edinburgh by T. G. Stevenson) is composed of rough quatrains closely resembling no 350. I cannot find the originals of nos 350–352 in either of his surviving works, however, and assume that they must be taken from some work of his that has perished.

Ten poems in the Section devoted to "Old Hymns of the *English* Church" remain to be attributed to their authors: nos 422–426 and 427–430 (which are marked off as separate groups by the sign † appended to no 422, no 427, and no 431), and no 431 itself; which is signed "[*Masters*]."

UNIDENTIFIED POEMS   I have not discovered the author of nos 422–426 or the author of nos 427–430; the first line of each of these pieces and the whole of no 427 are printed in Appendix G.

COWLEY   The last piece in the Section, no 431, presents no difficulty. It is headed "Ἄλις ἐνθέου Φλυάρου Κ.Τ.λ. and consists of four irregular *cola* of 13, 10, 10, and 18 lines. The signature "Masters" gives the clue: Thomas Master, or Masters, of New College (1603–43) was a celebrated composer in Greek as well as in Latin; his poem on the game of shovel-board, *Mensa Lubrica* (1641), was a prototype of the sets of Latin verses on homely contemporary topics that found a place in Anglo-Latin anthologies for more than a century,[42] and his Greek Ode on the Crucifixion, composed in 1633, was pub-

---

[42] See L. Bradner, *Musae Anglicanae*, 1940, p 204.

lished at Oxford[43] in 1658; it appeared[44] on p 28–29 of a collection of pieces by Sir Henry Savile and others, *D. Henrici Savilii* τοῦ μακαρίτου *Oratio . . . Aliaeque Doctiss: Virorum Opellae posthumae*, where it is dated "April 19 1633" and is followed by a Latin translation signed "H.I." (Henry Jacob, Fellow of Merton) and by Cowley's English version, which is unsigned. Cowley acknowledged his authorship of this translation by reprinting it in his *Verses written on Several Occasions*, 1663,[45] and it must have become widely known by reason of its reproduction in the long series of folios of his *Works* which began with the edition of 1668.

Cowley's poem consists of five *cola*; Gambold (or the author whose version he prints) has considerably abridged and slightly altered the first of these; he has reproduced the second and third almost *verbatim*; and he has omitted five lines from the beginning of Cowley's fourth *colon* and tacked on to the end of it three of the eleven lines of his fifth.

The following comparison shows the extent to which Gambold has adapted Cowley's opening *colon*:

COWLEY	MORAVIAN COLLECTION Part I no 431
Enough, my Muse, of Earthly things,	
And inspirations but of wind,	
Take up thy Lute, and to it bind	
Loud and everlasting strings;	
And on 'em play, and to 'em sing,	
The happy mournful stories,	Enough thou'st sung of Earth! now sing
The Lamentable glories,	The happy mournful Stories,
Of the great Crucified King.	The Lamentable glories,
Mountainous heap of wonders! which dost rise	Of the great crucified King.
Till Earth thou joynest with the Skies!	Mountainous Heap of wonders —
Too large at bottom, and at top too high,	Too large at bottom, and at top too high,
To be half seen by mortal eye.	To be half seen by mortal eye.
How shall I grasp this boundless thing?	How shall I grasp this boundless thing!
How shall I play? what shall I sing?	What shall I play? what shall I sing?

---

[43] "By Dr. Barlow," according to Wood's pencil note on the title-page of the Bodleian copy — Wood 512 (4).

[44] With the title Εἰς τήν τοῦ χριστοῦ σταύρωσιν Μονοστροφικα.

[45] With the title *Christs Passion, Taken out of a Greek Ode, written by* Mr. Masters *of New College* in Oxford.

APPENDIX A: Herbert [46]

MORAVIAN COLLECTION		*The Temple*
353 (W 28)	=	*The Agonie* (H 37) stanzas 2, 3 [3]
354	=	*An Offering* (H 147) stanza 4, abridged [7]
355	=	*Sunday* (H 75) stanzas 5, 6, 9, each slightly abridged [9]
356	=	*H. Baptisme* (H 43) [14 lines]
357	=	*The H. Communion* (H 52) stanza 2 [4]
358	=	*Give me my captive soul* (H 52) [4]
359	=	*Good Friday* (H 38) stanzas 1, 4, 5 [5]
360 (W 96)	=	*The Dawning* (H 112) each stanza slightly abridged [2]
361	=	*Whitsunday* (H 59) stanzas 1, 2, 7 [7]
362	=	*Ungratefulnesse* (H 82) each stanza slightly abridged [5]
363	=	*Decay* (H 99) each stanza slightly abridged [4]
364 (W 31)	=	*Mattens* (H 62) [5]
365 (W 33)	=	*The Elixir* (H 184) stanzas 1, 4, 5 (with Wesley's second stanza substituted for stanzas 2 and 3) [6]
366	=	*Evensong* (H 63) stanzas 2–4 [4]
367	=	*Businesse* (H 113) abridged to six 4-line stanzas [38 lines]
368 (W 47)	=	*Grieve not the Holy Spirit* (H 135) stanzas 1, 2, 6, each slightly abridged [6]
369 (W 73)	=	*Longing* (H 148) stanzas 3–8 loosely paraphrased, preceded by an imported stanza [14]
370 (W 70)	=	*Home* (H 107) stanzas 1–13 with an original stanza substituted for stanzas 7–9 [13]
371 (W 113)	=	*Praise II* (H 146) stanzas 1–5, 7 abridged to three 7-line stanzas [7]
372	=	*Constancie* (H 72) each stanza abridged [7]
373	=	*Affliction II* (H 62) each stanza slightly abridged [3]
374	=	*Marie Magdalene* (H 173) [3]
375	=	*The Bag* (H 151) stanzas 2, 4–7 [7]
376	=	*The Call* (H 156) [3]
377 (W 125)	=	*The Invitation* (H 179) stanzas 1–4, stanzas 3 and 4 transposed [6]
378 (W 126)	=	*The Banquet* (H 181) stanzas 1–6, 9, abridged and altered [9]

Harvey's *The Synagogue*

379	=	*The Circumcision* each stanza abridged [8]
380	=	*The Epiphany* [8]
381	=	*Whitsunday* stanzas 4, 5, 7, 8, 10, each abridged [10]
382	=	*Inmates* stanzas 1, 2, 5, 7–9, 11, 14, 15, each slightly abridged [15]

[46] The figures between round brackets indicate the page-numbers in Wesley's *Hymns and Sacred Poems*, 1739, and in Hutchinson's edition of Herbert's *Works*; those between square brackets, the number of stanzas (or lines) in the poem to the title of which they are appended.

APPENDIX B: Crashaw

MORAVIAN COLLECTION		Crashaw's *Poems* [47]
393	=	*On the Blessed Virgin's Bashfulnesse* (89) 8 lines abridged to 4
394	=	*I am the Doore* (90) 6 lines abridged to 2
395 [48]	=	*The Antiphona* (for *Compline* in *The Office of the Holy Crosse*) (275) 13 lines abridged to 10
396	=	*On the still surviving markes of our Saviour's wounds* (86) 10 lines abridged to 6
397 [48]	=	*The Antiphona* (for the *Third, Sixth,* and *Ninth Hours* in The Office of the Holy *Crosse*) (269, 270, 272)
398	=	*On the wounds of our crucified Lord* (99) [five stanzas] stanzas 1, 3, 4
399	=	*Upon the Bleeding Crucifix* (288) [nine stanzas and a concluding couplet] stanzas 1, 4, 3, 5, 9
400	=	*Vexilla Regis* (277) [seven stanzas and a concluding quatrain] stanzas 1–3, 5, 6
401	=	*Charitas Nimia* (280) 66 lines abridged to six 4-line stanzas
402	=	*Adoro Te* (292) lines 1–4, 39–54 followed by stanza 13 of *Lauda Sion Salvatorem* (294)

APPENDIX C: Donne

MORAVIAN COLLECTION		Donne: *Holy Sonnets* and *The Litanie*
383 stanzas 1–3	=	Sonnet I lines 1–12
stanza 4 line 1	=	Sonnet I line 14
2	=	Sonnet II line 14
3	=	Sonnet II line 13
4	=	Sonnet I line 13 (altered)
stanzas 5–7	=	Sonnet II lines 1–12 (line 12 altered)
stanzas 8–9	=	Sonnet XI lines 1–8
stanza 10	=	Sonnet XI lines 9–12 (lines 11 and 12 transposed)
stanza 11 line 1	=	no counterpart
lines 2 & 3	=	Sonnet XI lines 13, 14
line 4	=	no counterpart
stanzas 12, 13	=	Sonnet XIII lines 1–8
stanza 14 line 1	=	Sonnet XIII line 13
line 2	=	Sonnet XIII line 11
line 3	=	Sonnet XIII line 12
line 4	=	Sonnet XIII line 14
384 stanzas 1–6	=	*The Litanie,* stanzas 1–3

[47] Figures in round brackets indicate the page-number in Professor Martin's edition (Clarendon Press 1927); references in square brackets give the number of stanzas in the poem to the title of which they are appended.

[48] These pieces are evidently taken from the 1648 edition of *Steps to the Temple,* in which the Antiphons are printed as poems separate from the rest of the Office.

APPENDIX D: Faithfull Teate [49]

[49] The alterations throughout are considerable, save in no 391.
[50] I have used the second edition, 1669.
[51] Part only of stanza.
[52] Parts only of stanzas 147, 148.

APPENDIX E: Jeremy Taylor

APPENDIX F: Sir Matthew Hale

APPENDIX G: Unidentified Pieces

422   How wrapt am I, how full of bliss (23 four-line stanzas)
423   O Bless'd be God for ever blest! (42 four-line stanzas)
424   O vile and inconsid'rate man (28 four-line stanzas)
425   'Tis true indeed that for a while (29 four-line stanzas)
426   Why, O my Brother, art thou sad (19 four-line stanzas)
427   Remember how, (beside the bands
        Wherewith they bound him) thy Lord's hands
        And feet were pierc'd, that thence might flow
        The Salve for sin-procured Woe:
        That thou of its near Droppings ne'er mayst fail,
        Refuse not to be fasten'd with his Nail.
428   Thy Saviour press'd to death, there ran (3 four-line stanzas)
429   On thee, my sure Foundation (3 four-line stanzas)
430   What a blessed change I find (6 six-line stanzas)

NOTE: For the sake of completeness, note 30, page 13, may be amplified; Benson (66–67) says, "[Herbert's] actual connection with Hymnody came through the appearance in 1697 of *Select Hymns from Mr Herbert's Temple*, in which a C.M. recension of some of his verses was attempted, and through his later influence upon the Wesleys." *Select Hymns* now exists, it appears, only in one copy, that in Dr Williams's Library, London Square, London. Professor William E. Stephenson of the University of California, editor of *Select Hymns* (Los Angeles, Augustan Reprint Society No 98 1962) has been unable to identify the adapter who was responsible for the selection, but shows that he must have been a Dissenter, and suggests that he was one of the many divines whose poems and sermons were published by Thomas Parkhurst, publisher of this selection. Thirty-two of Herbert's poems are "Turn'd into the Common Metre. To be sung in the tunes ordinarily us'd in Churches." Eight of the 32 were also adapted in the Moravian Collection of 1754, but a comparison of the texts reveals no reason for supposing that Gambold had ever seen *Select Hymns, 1697*.   J.S.

A
COLLECTION
OF
H Y M N S
OF THE
CHILDREN of GOD in all Ages,

From the Beginning till now.

In Two PARTS.

Defigned chiefly for the Ufe of the CONGREGATIONS

In Union with the

BRETHREN's CHURCH.

Speaking to yourfelves in Pfalms and Hymns and fpiritual Songs, finging and making Melody in your Heart to the Lord. Eph. v. 19.

L O N D O N

Printed; and to be had at all the Brethren's Chapels.

M DCC LIV.

Title page of the Moravian *Collection.*   *Union Theological Seminary Library*

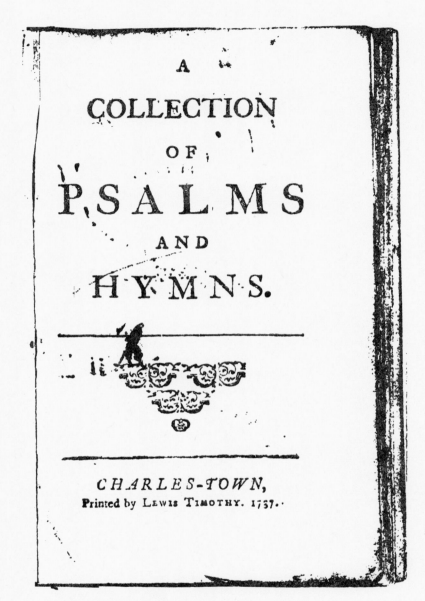

A

COLLECTION

OF,

PSALMS

AND

HYMNS.

CHARLES-TOWN,
Printed by Lewis Timothy. 1737.

A Collection of Psalms and Hymns (Charleston, S C 1737).

The First Wesley Hymn Book

A SMALL VOLUME in the Rare Book Division of The New York Public Library is a bibliographical item interesting for its rarity. It is also a souvenir, a memento of the passions and problems of a crucial time in a great life. *A Collection of Psalms and Hymns* was compiled by John Wesley during his stay in Georgia and published in Charleston, South Carolina, in 1737.

Wesley's *Georgia Journal* tells of the making of the book, and of life as lived by an Oxford don lately turned pioneer. Biographers take pleasure in associating the various hymns with the particular triumphs and disappointments of that rigorous life, and the *Collection* itself played a part in determining his fate in the New World. The book is the first significant publication of either of the famous brothers. And, apart from its bibliographical and biographical interest, it has importance in the history of the English hymn as a literary genre.

On October 14 1735 John and Charles Wesley boarded the *Simmonds* to sail with Governor Oglethorpe as missionary clergymen sent out by the Church of England to the colonies. Aboard were twenty-six members of the Moravian Brotherhood, on their way to join others of their sect who had earlier colonized in North America. The sect had broken from the governance and discipline of the Lutheran church; from the persecutions that resulted, they had been given refuge on the estate of Count Nicolaus Ludwig von Zinzendorf in Bohemia, in a settlement called Herrnhuth.

Wesley's journal for October 17 records, "I began to learn German, in order to converse with the Moravians." [1] On the 20th he began to teach English to three of the group. From the 21st on he joined them in their daily religious services conducted in German. On the 27th he notes: "began Gesang-Buch." By January he conversed and read easily in German.

They landed February 6 1736. The next day he met Spangenberg, pastor of the Moravians in Georgia. In March he began his correspondence with

---

[1] *The Journal of John Wesley*, ed Nehemiah Curnock et al, 11 vols (1960) i 110. The eleventh volume is in preparation.

Zinzendorf, quoting in his first letter a hymn by the Count which he later translated.[2]

March 24 he moved on to the third section of *Das Gesang Buch*. May 2 he began the study of formal grammar in German. May 10 he set down plans for the formation of societies in Savannah and Frederica in which song was to play as large a part as it played in Moravian services.

Some Spanish Jews lived in his parish, and on Monday June 18 he started to learn Spanish so he could converse with them, Dr Nunes being his chief instructor. On Friday of that week he "Sung Spanish verses," possibly the Spanish version of Psalm LXIII which he published in his own translation in his second collection in 1738.[3] From July 5, he often noted: "Singing George Herbert." He was testing the hymn versions of *The Temple* and testing his translations, singing them with friends, at meetings of the societies, and alone.

Part of the time he had a housekeeper to aid in entertaining his many official guests, but part of the time he kept his own house, made his garden, fished for food for the guests. Storms on sea and land, journeys in fierce heat and cold through primitive land on foot, boat trips when water and food gave out, death-watches in time of epidemics were part of life. If he became ill, his cures were fasting and the felling of trees. He performed marriages, baptized babies, buried the dead, conducted his work as secretary to Governor Oglethorpe, his preaching, his conferences with the Indians, the state correspondence and his own.

He learned John Byrom's method of short-hand, abandoning his private cipher so Charles could read his diaries. He read Italian, worked intensively in Spanish, taught French, Greek, German, Hebrew, human anatomy, church history, canon law. He read Latin with the other divines, played on the flute, read Milton, Watts, Herbert, wrote a French grammar, an English grammar, a German grammar, a German dictionary, a book of prayers, a book of catechisms, some of his best known sermons, condensations from his endless reading of learned tomes in many languages, much of which material he later published. Bewildered by his love affair, he coped with women, petty politics, deep questions of theology and practical problems of missionary life.

Travels on foot were pretext for doctrinal discussions: "conversed. . . . Walked together; bemired. Lost; return . . . bemired. Lost; prayed; found

---

[2] James T[aft] Hatfield, "John Wesley's Translations of German Hymns," *PMLA* XI No 2 (1896) 1–29. Mr Hatfield discovered the letter in the archives at Herrnhuth.

[3] *The Poetical Works of John and Charles Wesley* ed G[eorge] Osborn, 13 vols (1868–72) I 174. See also note II 38. Cited as *Osborn*.

way. Lost prayed; found way; lost again. Walking; tired. Lay down by a wood; slept sound." [4] His polyglot ministry went on as he conducted services in German, English, French, Spanish and Italian. Interpreting for foreign envoys was part of his state duties. He wrote his hymns, only momentarily deterred when the ink froze in the bottle, and wrote his *Georgia Journal,* subject of reams of praise and denunciation. He could parcel out even this life and record it hour by hour so methodically that there was time for everything, including what seems the teaching schedule of a one-man university faculty. But something worked like leaven within him, like the leaven hid in the three measures of meal, and he ejaculated, "O Discipline! where art thou to be found?" [5]

Charles Wesley was not involved in the work of hymnody. He left Georgia July 26 1736 to return to England and John accompanied him as far as Charleston. The diary does not mention it, but he may at this time have made preliminary arrangements with the printer Lewis Timothy to print the hymn collection. The book was not in proof until April of the next year. [6]

A Collection of Psalms and Hymns was in use soon after April 1737 in meetings of the societies. His hymn writing continued; he was preparing a second volume. On June 19 1737 his book was first used in a service of the Church of England. August 9 a warrant was issued for his arrest and he was haled into court on twelve charges, the first three being: he "deviates from the principles and regulations of the Established Church, in many particulars inconsistent with the happiness and prosperity of this Colony, as —

"Prima, by inverting the order and method of the Liturgy,

"2. By changing or altering such passages as he thinks proper in the versions of Psalms publicly authorized to be sung in church.

"3. By introducing into the church and service at the altar compositions of psalms and hymns not inspected or authorized by any proper judicature; . . . etc." [7]

The major cause of his accusers' wrath was "The Case of Sophy," Sophy being a very young lady whom John Wesley did not marry, who, upon being convinced that he did not want to marry her, had married a Mr Williams. Wesley, because of ecclesiastical reasons perhaps not unmixed with unpastoral annoyance at some of her actions, refused to give her the Holy Communion; whereupon her relatives, acting on motives perhaps not

[4] *Journal* I 268.
[5] *Journal* I 271.
[6] *Journal* I 349. Entry for April 18 1737.
[7] *Journal* I 385.

unmixed with human considerations, brought the twelve charges against him. Eleven of the charges were ecclesiastical, and these he refused to answer in a civil court. The twelfth charge, an allegation of slander, he made every effort to bring to trial. Failing in all his attempts to compel his enemies to prove the charge in court or retract it, he took counsel with his friends and decided to return to England. He sailed from Charleston aboard the *Samuel* on December 24 1737 and arrived in England on February 1 1738.

In 1738 he published another book with the same title, like the American collection anonymous, and like it divided into three sections, hymns for Sunday (suited to general worship), for Wednesday and Friday (confession and humiliation), and for Saturday (praise to God especially considered as the Creator of the Universe). The organization based on the ancient way of offices may indicate a hope that the Established Church would accept hymnody. If so (and this is not necessarily true, for books of devotion had this organization), he was disappointed, for the Anglican Church did not really welcome hymnody before about the middle of the nineteenth century. All later Wesley hymn books were prepared for use outside the sanctuary.

In 1739 he and Charles published under their own names the first joint product, *Hymns and Sacred Songs*, many times expanded and reissued.

In 1741 they used the same title of John's first two books for a joint publication. *A Collection of Psalms and Hymns* by John and Charles Wesley had a second edition in 1743, and the many subsequent editions were numbered consecutively without regard for the two earlier books published by John alone.

And so when George Osborn edited the poetical works of the two brothers (13 vols; 1868–1872), he puzzled over a brief autobiographical account written by John Wesley on March 15 1740 for insertion in a new and enlarged edition of Wood's *Athenae Oxoniensis*, which states that he published "a Collection of Psalms and Hymns in 1736." The American publication was completely unknown. The collection of 1738 is very rare, only two copies being known to exist, one at Didsbury College in Bristol, one in Lambeth Palace. Wesley did not mention two collections, and Osborn concluded that Wesley had made a mistake (as indeed he had), and that the entry referred to the 1738 collection. His edition of the poems, therefore, makes no mention of a publication before 1738.

In 1882 a copy of the first collection was found in a London book store. A few months later Osborn issued a reprint with his preface giving some analysis of the contents of the book and a provenance and history of the volume. This is supposed to have been Wesley's own copy, for no other is known to have reached London. Since 1936 it has been in the Methodist archives in London.

A second copy of the book came into the possession of Alexander Maitland, grand-nephew of James Lenox, whose collection formed the nucleus of The New York Public Library's Rare Book Division. Mr Maitland gave the book to the Library in 1899. The last page was accidentally left blank by the printer, the catch-word appearing on the previous page 73. The book is endorsed, "M. Tiddeman, May 20, 17—," possibly 1791. The full table of its contents is given at the end of this chapter.

The predominance of the lyrics of Isaac Watts — 35 of the 70 songs being his — does not indicate that Wesley in the wilds of Georgia lacked other material; thirty-six of the 76 songs in his second collection published in England were from Watts. Although Watts had predecessors in the writing of the English hymn, and wrote in response to a demand for hymnody which had existed among Dissenting congregations for some time,[8] his claim to the title, the Father of English Hymnody, is secure. His "grand design" for the renovation of congregational singing was published in two books, *The Psalms of David Imitated*, and *Hymns and Spiritual Songs*. His versions of the psalms were not translations, but imitations which rendered them in Christian terminology and placed the supposed speaker in Britain and in circumstances appropriate to that day, as Samuel Johnson rendered Juvenal's satire in his poem *London*. The hymns were in three divisions, the first book being based on specific scriptures for congregations who wished to sing only songs written in this manner, the second book being free-composed hymns, the third book being hymns to be sung at the Lord's Supper and doxologies. Wesley drew on all these types of songs. Watts published also another volume of poems, *Horae Lyricae*, with lyrics on similar religious subjects and in hymn meters, but using metaphoric interpretations of the scriptures too "bold" for ordinary congregational use.

There was a peculiar oneness of spirit between the most celebrated Dissenter of the day and the High Church Wesleys. Both Charles and John set out for eternity with Watts hymns on their lips. Even in discussions of predestination and election, the Arminian Wesleys drew the writings of the Calvinist Watts over to their side.[9] For certain types of hymns Watts has

[8] Louis Benson, *The English Hymn* (1960) 19–107; John Julian, *A Dictionary of Hymnology* (1957) I 343–350.

[9] *Journal* II 473. John Wesley's selections from Watts's writings were published as *Serious Consideration Concerning the Doctrines of Election and Reproduction Extracted from a Late Author*, 6th ed (1813). Much of this material is found in Robert Southey's *Life of Watts*, often bound in copies of *Horae Lyricae*.

never been surpassed in English, and Wesley hymnody counted on him
for those types. His clear and perspicuous statements of classic Christian
doctrine set in poetic style suited to the taste of the Age of Reason and
Common Sense were always part of their public song and private devotions. Before the brothers brought out their first joint hymnal, they visited
Dr Watts and the three "walked and sang" together.[10] His vision of the
majesty of God and his consecration to that vision are the refined gold of
Calvinism. By his advocacy of hymns he flouted an opinion (never a dogma)
of Calvin, but in his songs is the insignia of Calvin's personal crest: a hand
reaching up, in the palm a burning heart, with the words, "I give thee all."
In him was a wide and deep religious toleration, learned, he said, from
John Locke. *Joy* is his key word, and "Joy to the world" perhaps his best-
known song. From his free-composed hymns Wesley chose for this first
collection a song now sung in the South to a tune that might stretch even
Dr Watts's concept of sacred joy: "Come ye that love the Lord, and let
your joys be known," merriest of the church's come-all-ye's, and gay as the
street ballads on which it was modeled. And, in this book foretelling a hymnody that would come from Charles, and would place greater reliance on
image and symbol, John boldly chose two songs from *Horae Lyricae.*

The collection of 1737 emphasizes the fact that John, not Charles, took
the lead in hymnody. His use of writings from his father and his older
brother testifies to the powerful cohesion of the family group, but it was
not a cohesion without controversy. The father was dead, but the brother
lived until 1739. His aversion to Watts's psalmody and to his urging of the
use of spontaneous prayer in church services is a matter of record,[11] as is
his impatience with the Methodist tendencies of his two younger brothers.[12]
As private devotions the writings of the Roman Catholic John Austin and
the Whig Addison might be acceptable, but any variation of the service of
the Established Church would have seemed disreputable to him, and this
collection with its robust eclecticism must have seemed a strange amalgam
for a Wesley to offer to the Church.

In compiling his collection, Wesley was searching for a quality which is
not prominent in Watts, a warmth of subjective emotional expression which

---

10 *Journal* II 82.

11 Samuel Wesley, M.A. Jun., *Poems on Several Occasions* ed James Nichols (1862) 356–358.
Two satiric poems addressed to Watts, "On the Forms of Prayer," "Upon Altering the Psalms
to Apply Them to a Christian State."

12 James T. Lightwood, "A Note on Samuel Wesley," *Wesley Historical Society Proceedings* II
(1898) 55–56. Lightwood (who is the authority on hymn tunes) cites a letter in the Bodleian
Library; he does not give the name of the addressee.

Charles was soon to give him in rich supply. At this time he sought the quality from two sources, George Herbert and the German hymns. The tides of taste, moving by their own inexplicable laws, turned against Herbert early in the century. *The Temple*, which had been sanctuary indeed for all factions in the wars of the seventeenth century, had a thirteenth edition in 1709, and was not reissued for ninety years. Canon Hutchinson, editor of Herbert, says that Wesley more than any other man helped fill the gap during the lean years.[13] His hymn versions of Herbert went through many editions. He included Herbert in collections for devotional reading, two of the poems in strange form labeled "Anacreontick." Canon Hutchinson thought them John's contrivances; but one is surely the work of his brother Samuel, for it appears in his collected poems,[14] and the other is almost certainly his also. In 1753 Wesley published Walton's *Life of Herbert* in his popular series *A Christian Library*, and in 1773 published in that series the only considerable body of Herbert's poetry to appear in its original form during the ninety-year period. That the hymn alterations do not suit our poetic taste is beside the point; Herbert unaltered did not suit the taste of 1737. John, a realist, could recognize a trend, but the history of his own publications of Herbert shows where his preference lay. He moved toward the original poems, and led many followers with him, back to the favorite poet of that remarkable mother of his. Popular for a time, Wesley's hymn adaptations of Herbert went out of use in John's lifetime. Charles Wesley's hymns supplied the needed quality, and Herbert was returned to his proper place in the secret heart. No attempt to make Herbert "choral" has been successful, not even Ralph Vaughan Williams' freer anthem forms. Perhaps the most unmistakable individual voice in English poetry, Herbert is not choric, but the superlative of solo. That his voice is able to speak for all kinds and conditions of men is his miracle, but it is not a miracle that lies within the genre of the hymn. Alteration was necessary to bring the poems within the hymn genre. The first five of Wesley's 47 adaptations appeared in this book, and the many subsequent publications at least kept the name before the public.

When church services were put into the vernacular at the time of the Reformation, the churches under Luther's influence sang hymns. The Gregorian reformation of church music in the sixth century, which confined

---

[13] F. E. Hutchinson, "John Wesley and George Herbert," *London Quarterly and Holborn Review* (October 1936) 439–455.

[14] S. Wesley, 224. Cf John Wesley, *A Collection of Moral and Sacred Poems* 3 vols (1744) III 86, 139.

singing to clerical choirs, was never carried out in Germany as strictly as in other places, and there was an intermittent tradition of congregational singing. Luther fostered hymnody; the songs increased during the Golden Age of German hymnody until, when Bach began to arrange them into his chorales, all of which are arranged from popular hymns, there were at least 8,427 hymns in print for him to draw on,[15] including the work of Paul Gerhardt, called by Albert Schweitzer the king of hymnwriters.[16]

Calvin found no tradition of congregational song; and he had to battle another "tradition" of court singing of sacred texts mingled with material which can more accurately be called licentious than popular. He feared to leave so important an aspect of ecclesiastical conduct to the discretion of the generality of the clergy at that time, and he restricted congregational singing to the 150 canonical psalms, the Ten Commandments, the Lord's Prayer, a few New Testament canticles (if indeed these were sung in church; liturgiologists are undecided), and the fourth century Te Deum. These were set in rhymed stanzaic form, a mnemonic aid to congregations in which few could read. Using the best artists available, he produced in the Geneva Psalter a work of grave and impressive beauty, surpassing in richness and metrical subtlety any English authorized version. For England followed Calvin in this matter. Early attempts to introduce Lutheran principles of hymnody by Myles Coverdale in England and the Wedderburns in Scotland were suppressed. When Watts published *Hymns and Spiritual Songs* in 1707, with few exceptions, Anglican and Dissenter alike sang metrical psalms. From this ruling arose the charges brought against Wesley for his use of hymns and unauthorized psalm versions.

Watts had heard of the singing in Germany, and he invoked it as an inspiration in his revolutionizing of English church music, but he could not read German, and Germanic studies in England were nonexistent in 1737 when John Wesley introduced into English the first influence of German hymnody.[17] His German hymns were soon in use in all congregations that allowed the use of hymns, were adopted as hymnody was adopted, and remain in wide popular use and high critical esteem. When Coleridge and Carlyle (himself a bringer-in of Lutheran hymnody) focused attention on

---

[15] Stainton de B. Taylor, *The Chorale Preludes of J. S. Bach* (1944), p 3.

[16] Albert Schweitzer, *Johann Sebastian Bach* 2 vols (1944) ɪ 12.

[17] Twenty-nine hymns were published. Another was printed only in the *Journal* ɪ 299, identified *Journal* ɪɪ 6 by Dr Henry Bett. Dr Frank Baker, *Representative Verse of Charles Wesley* (1962) 4–5, discusses the possibility of Charles's authorship of a translation of J. Scheffler's "Dich, Jesu, loben wir," usually attributed to John Wesley. J. T. Hatfield's essay noted above is an excellent discussion of the German hymns.

Germanic studies, the reputation of Wesley's translations reached new heights. Emerson and Holmes declared "Thou hidden love of God" the finest hymn in the English language. Henry Ward Beecher so far exaggerated the German influence as to say that German hymnody was "the fountain in which Charles Wesley was baptized." The statement appears in the preface (page v) to his *Plymouth Collection* (1855), a hymn book which marks the extreme departure of a devout Calvinist from Calvin's position on church music, for it embraces many writings from lay authors who held themselves responsible to speak the truth as they felt it, but responsible to no dogmatic authority.

And the collection of 1737 is perhaps most important in its revelation of the duties of an editor of hymn books as viewed by this greatest of all such editors. John Wesley altered almost every lyric in the book. He compressed Watts into even more succinct form. Watts's Psalm C, for example, appears here as it usually is seen in modern hymnals, stanzas 1 and 4 omitted, stanza 2 altered to bestow upon one of Watts's most popular songs a purely Wesley title, "Before Jehovah's awful throne." Zinzendorf's hymn, placed beside its original, can be recognized with difficulty.

From its inception, the English hymn as a genre has operated on a principle of diction which is peculiar to itself. The rule is: If you don't like it, change it. Hymns are partly in the oral tradition, in that their true purpose is not fulfilled unless they are vocalized. They are not, however, altered by oral transmission, as ballads were, for the text of the hymn exists before the eyes. Alteration is done by editors to suit current needs and taste. Often it is done very badly, but the rule remains in force, for hymns must be altered. There are today certain figures of speech which do not edify modern congregations, however they may be authenticated by the King James Version. The late Bernard L. Manning was both a devotee and a purist, yet he said some lines by Watts could make him cringe.[18] The lines made no one cringe when they were written; no offense was intended.

The Father of English Hymnody blessed his infant genre at birth with this characteristic of mutability.

> If any Expression occurs to the Reader that savours of an Opinion different from his own, yet he may observe these are generally such as are capable of an extensive Sense, and may be us'd with a charitable Latitude. Tho' I don't pretend this is the properest Method to write Treatises of Divinity which are to be read in private; yet I think 'tis most agreeable, that what is provided for publick Worship shou'd give

[18] Bernard Lord Manning, *The Hymns of Wesley and Watts* (1960) 86.

to sincere Consciences as little Vexation and Disturbance as possible. However, where any unpleasing Word is found, he that leads the Worship may substitute a better.

Wesley, in the preface of the definitive collection of Wesley hymns in 1780, asked that his brother's verses be not thus altered. He meant to pay tribute to his brother's stature as poet and theologian. But Charles Wesley was a greater poet than even his brother knew. His is a work which the world will not let die, and which the world will not let alone. Julian's *Dictionary of Hymnology* lists 17 variants of "Jesu, Lover of my soul," and mentions many more. C. D. Hardcote, writing in 1898, said he listed 157 variant versions of the song from books in his own library.

Almost every application of this rule causes distress to some member of a congregation, but even purists agree that some things must be changed. The result of insistence upon absolute purity of text would be to end one of the lives of some great hymns, and relegate them to rare book rooms, where the pure texts live another, quieter life. Editors can refer to them there, and the process of change includes restoration as well as elision. Editors in the future may restore the references to worms and the bowels of compassion which are vexation and disturbance to the delicacy of this not especially delicate age we live in, but they will remove the unpredictable offenses which may arise in future generations.

This rule makes possible what the collection of 1737 demonstrates: the usefulness of material from many shades of religious opinion. Watts marked the genre as author, Wesley marked it as editor, with a catholicity of spirit which can be seen in hymnals, where songs written by Quakers and songs from synagogues, from Unitarians and Roman Catholics, Greek hymns from antiquity and folk songs from central Europe attain harmony. It is an in-joke among hymnologists that the hymns of Watts and the Wesleys reformed the Reformation. John Wesley was the greatest of all hymn editors, and the collection of 1737 is the first in-gathering of his catholic spirit.

APPENDIX: Contents of *A Collection of Psalms and Hymns* 1737

1

Psalms and Hymns for Sunday

1   Psalm XXXIII   [Watts] [19]
2   Psalm XLVI [20]

[19] Isaac Watts, *The Psalms of David Imitated in the Language of the New Testament* (1719). All psalm versions by Watts are from this book.
[20] See extended note, page 148 below.

3   Psalm XLVII [Watts]
4   Psalm C [Watts]
5   Psalm CXIII [Samuel Wesley the Elder]
6   Psalm CXV [Samuel Wesley the Elder]
7   Psalm CXVI [Samuel Wesley the Elder]
8   Psalm CXVII [Samuel Wesley the Elder]
9   Psalm CXLVI [Watts]
10   Psalm CXLVII [Watts]
11   Hymn to God the Father [Samuel Wesley the Younger]
12   Hymn to God the Son [Samuel Wesley the Younger]
13   Hymn to God the Holy-Ghost [Samuel Wesley the Younger]
14   Hymn to the Trinity [Samuel Wesley the Younger]
15   God's Eternity [Watts, Hymns, Bk II no 17] [21]
16   From the German [of Ernest Lange, "O Gott, du tieffe sonder grund!" *Das Gesang-Buch der Herrnhuth* (1731), no 16. Also in *Evangelischer Liederschatz*, ed A. Knapp (1865), no 1. Wesley's translation in a slightly altered version is in Osborn 1 143]
17   Hymn to Christ [Austin, Hymn 31] [22]
18   Adoption [Watts, Hymn, Bk I no 64]
19   The Christian Race [Watts, Hymn, Bk I no 48]
20   Praise [George Herbert. Wesley's adaptation, Osborn 1 102]
21   Christ's Humiliation and Exaltation [Watts, Hymn, Bk I no 63]
22   Hymn to the Holy-Ghost [Austin, Hymn 35]
23   The Offices of Christ [Watts, Hymns, Bk II no 132]
24   Hymn for Sunday [Austin, Hymn 1]
25   Triumph over Death [Watts, Hymns, Bk II no 110]
26   From the German [of Zinzendorf, "Reiner Braut'gam meiner Seele," *Das Gesang-Buch*, no 982, Knapp, no 1830. Wesley's translation, Osborn 1 107]
27   Thanksgiving for God's Particular Providence [Joseph Addison, *Spectator* no 453. "When all thy mercies, O my God"]
28   A Morning Hymn [Watts, Hymns, Bk I no 81]
29   Heaven Begun on Earth [Watts, Hymns, Bk II no 30]
30   The Names of Christ [Watts, Hymns, Bk I no 149]
31   Solomon's Song, Ch 2 Ver 8 &c [Watts, Hymns, Bk I no 69]
32   Verse 14, &c [Watts, Hymns, Bk I no 70]
33   Sincere Praise [Watts, *Horae Lyricae*, Bk I 23rd poem (the songs are not numbered)]
34   O ye Spirits and Souls of the Righteous, bless ye the Lord [Austin, Hymn 37]
35   The Shortness of Life [Watts, Hymns, Bk II no 58]
36   Christ our Wisdom, &c [Watts, Hymns, Bk I no 97]
37   Gloria Patri [Watts, Hymns, Bk III no 26]
38   Hymn to Christ [Austin, Hymn 30]
39   Prayer ["Prayer II," Herbert. Wesley's adaptation, Osborn 1 124]
40   From the German [of J. A. Freylinghausen, "Wer ist wohl, wie du." *Das Gesang-Buch*, no 42. Knapp, no 268. Wesley's translation, Osborn 1 161]

[21] Isaac Watts, *Hymns and Spiritual Songs* 2nd ed (1709). The second edition was enlarged. All Watts's hymns are located in this volume by number.

[22] John Austin, *Devotions in the Antient Way of Offices* 2nd ed (1672). Austin's book was first published in Paris in 1668. It had four editions in the Roman form, and was twice altered for Anglican use. Wesley used the Anglican version made by Lady Susannah Hopton, and published with a preface by George Hickes D.D. It is often referred to as "Hickes' Reformed Devotions." It "hath not left out, or altered anything" in Austin's book "but some few Sentences, and Expressions, which hinder'd those Offices from being introduc'd into the Closets, and Oratories, of the more devout Sons, and Daughters of the Church of England." Austin's first edition contained 39 hymns, his third 43. Hickes gives 40.

2

Psalms and Hymns for Wednesday and Friday

1   Psalm XXXVIII   [Watts]
2   Psalm LI   [Watts]
3   Psalm XC   [Watts, L. M.]
4   Psalm XC   [Watts, C. M., second part] [23]
5   A Thought in Affliction [24]
6   On the Crucifixion   [Samuel Wesley the Younger]
7   Discipline   [Herbert. Wesley's adaptation, Osborn i 69]
8   On the Crucifixion   [Samuel Wesley the Elder]
9   A Sinner's Prayer   [made up from two poems by Herbert, "Complaining" and "Grieve not the Holy Spirit." Correctly separated in later publications into two poems. Herbert's titles restored; see Osborn i 43 and 63]
10   Judgment   [Joseph Addison, *Spectator*, no 513. "When rising from the Bed of Death"]
11   Christ's Compassion to the Tempted   [Watts, Hymns, Bk I no 125]
12   Frailty   [Herbert. Wesley's adaptation, Osborn i 37]
13   Unfruitfulness   [Watts, Hymns, Bk II no 165]
14   From the German   [of C. F. Richter, "Stilles Lamm und Friede-Fürst." *Das Gesang-Buch*, no 989; Knapp, no 1665. Wesley's translation, Osborn i 129]
15   Faith in Christ   [Watts, Hymns, Bk II no 90]
16   Longing   [Herbert. Wesley's adaptation Osborn i 66]
17   Salvation by Grace   [Watts, Hymns, Bk I no 111]
18   Inconstancy   [3 of the 12 stanzas of Austin, Hymn 4, slightly altered. A quatrain by John Wesley is added. This, beginning "Guide Thou, my Lord, guide Thou my Course," is thought to be the only original work in this book by John Wesley]
19   Christ our Righteousness   [Watts, Hymns, Bk I no 98]
20   From the German   [of C. F. Richter, "Hier legt mein Sinn sich vor dir nieder," *Das Gesang-Buch*, no 1037; Knapp, no 1612. Wesley's translation, Osborn i 85]

3

Psalms and Hymns for Saturday

1   Psalm XIX   [Watts, S. M.]
2   The same   [Joseph Addison, *Spectator*, no 465]
3   The same   [Watts, old 113th]
4   Psalm LXV   [Watts, L. M. second part]
5   Psalm CIV [20]
6   Psalm CXIV   [Watts]
7   Psalm CXLVIII [Watts, S. M.]
8   Universal Praise   [Austin, Hymn 6]
9   Sun, Moon and Stars, Praise ye the Lord   [Watts, *Horae Lyricae*, Bk I 21st song]
10   Eupolis's Hymn to the Creator   [Samuel Wesley the Elder] [25]

[23] Any modern compiler of a hymn book would have chosen Watts's Psalm XC, L.M., first part, in preference to the two sections Wesley chose; it is "O God, our help in ages past," a song which has become almost a second national anthem for England, Canada, and the United States.

[24] Printed by Osborn ii 4 as possibly by Wesley. Osborn is dubious, and Louis Benson apparently does not accept it as Wesley's; see *The English Hymn* p 226.

[25] John Julian, *A Dictionary of Hymnology* ii 1256 assigns the major part of this poem to the daughter Mehetabel. John Wesley elsewhere assigned it entirely to his father, however. He closed this book with it; he and Charles opened their first joint publication with it. See Osborn i 1 for that version and notes. In the collection of 1737 John altered it from the original meter to DLM. Some notes on Addison's hymns and his relation to Watts are given by Julian i 16–19.

Blake and the Hymns of Charles Wesley

INTEREST in Wesley and Blake was never higher. The large simplicities of historical generalization suggest that our day, feeling itself threatened by prose and abstraction, is interested in the two genuine singing voices of another age of prose and abstraction. The two provocative poets are the subjects of fine scholarship, intricate analysis, philosophical meditation. They are quoted on burning issues, enlisted in political and theological programs, sung by church choirs, college glee clubs, village choral societies. They offer an open field to any who will risk the self-exposure their study seems to entail. Northrop Frye, writing on Blake, and Bernard Manning, writing on Wesley, have warned of that risk. As the first to write on both poets, I shall doubtless reveal with double clarity all the dubious grounds for my opinions, and may as well say at once that I think Wesley as good a poet as Blake, that I accept the testimony of children and the church choir along with scholarly opinion, that I reason from the proof of poetry as it is useful in ordinary living.

Blake recorded his opinion of John Wesley and George Whitefield, two of the three men who in their youth bound themselves into a "three-fold cord" and later became the leaders of the evangelical revival. He never mentioned the third, Charles Wesley. I shall examine three books by Wesley produced over a period of forty years and three produced by Blake over a period of at least thirty-six years, and I have considered all their works and days as best I can in formulating my conclusions about the possibility of literary relationship.

We read poetry at varying distances. From a normal middle ground, the work of the two men displays many differences. From a very close view, many details are alike. There is a long view of art and life from which vantage point they seem to stand together and stand alone. Since clarity of vision may be impaired by too close or too distant a view, I shall revert often to the conventional position from which differences are clear and plain. I begin at a point where certain small likenesses are clear and plain.[1]

---

[1] Numbers in parentheses refer, respectively, to pages in *The Poetry and Prose of William Blake*, ed Erdman (New York 1965), or to volume and pages in *The Poetical Works of John and Charles Wesley*, ed Osborn, 13 vols (London 1868–72).

1 WESLEY'S HYMNS FOR CHILDREN AND BLAKE'S *SONGS*

CHARLES WESLEY died in 1788. In 1789 Blake etched the first version of *Songs of Innocence*, which begins with a child's request for "a song about a Lamb." That poem and "The Lamb" are written in "Wesley's hammerheaded iambics."

> He is meek & he is mild;
> He became a little child.
> I a child, & thou a lamb,
> We are called by his name. (9)

From 1742 on, Charles Wesley had taught thousands of children to sing:

> Gentle Jesus, meek and mild,
> Look upon a little child. (vi 441)
>
> Jesus, gentle loving Lamb,
> Let me call Thee by Thy name. (ii 97)

Throughout the Bible, the Lamb is central to interpretation.[1] The genius of Hebrew imagination fused this everyday reality of life with exalted myth.[2]

[1] The chief occupation of a pastoral people became an image of the relation between God and man. The daily work was caring for this helpless creature, source of necessary food and the unit of wealth. The firstlings of Abel's flocks were an acceptable sacrifice and symbol of the contrite heart. The vicarious nature of the sacrifice became emblematic of the bearing of sin and the removal of guilt. The holy sign of the Paschal Lamb was token of salvation to the sons of man. A heroic shepherd boy, his songs and his childish weapons triumphant over man, brute, and demonic powers, built Jerusalem and made it the earthly City of God. In city life, there came nostalgia for the pastoral life, and always the herding of flocks was kept, actually and emotionally, close to the City. David's son sang of the Shepherd-Bridegroom, and when Jesus was born of the house and lineage of David, his birth was announced to shepherds and theirs was the first act of worship. His ministry was announced, "Behold the lamb." He was sacrificial lamb and builder and maker and shepherd and bridegroom and saviour and prophet and priest and king. The terrible warrior of Revelation is the militant Lamb. The Regnant Lamb is Lord of the New Jerusalem and Judge of the Nations.

[2] I use the word myth to emphasize narrative sequence, *mythos*, as contrasted with image, symbol, doctrine; and to emphasize, with reference to the Bible, the classic Christian interpretation of the entire Bible as essentially one story. This interpretation of the Bible was held in common by Wesley and Blake. Blake did not in any way set the Old Testament below the New Testament in authority or sanctity; nor did he look upon any other myth (the Greek or Roman, for example) as being of equal status or value with the Bible (although compare Principle 6 and Principle 5 in *All Religions are One*). The word *history* will not serve my purpose, for Wesley and Blake did not share the same views on the historicity of the Bible. The word *legend* will not serve. Although myth has become a word fraught with controversy in modern criticism, I refuse to abandon a good, useful word. Blake and Wesley differed in many points of interpretation of the Bible; but this general interpretation was common to them both, and the idea of myth, in the sense of a comprehensive plot or narrative, is of prime importance in the reading of their poetry.

The material is pastoral, heroic, symbolic. Never before Charles Wesley wrote had this material been so concentrated in the world of the child. There are reasons why this should be so. During the Middle Ages, the church elevated the image of the Infant and the Mother. The folk art of song, dance, story and drama had an air of childish naïvete and sanctified even its horseplay by reference to this image. Reformation men, rebelling against a church that kept most grown men outside its serious proceedings by means of language, organization, and policy, came to fear childishness as representing a threat of a new enslavement with its concomitant wish to be enslaved. Puritans wanted children brought as early as possible to man's estate for the child's own good. Children were dressed like adults and urged toward adult freedoms and responsibilities. In English literature of this period, the figure of the child is not prominent, and the image of the child with the mother is even less in evidence. Strict Puritans associated elements that were popish, pagan, and superstitious with many childish activities. Even the celebration of the ecclesiastical year was thus viewed, especially the Birthday of the Child.[4]

John Locke greatly influenced ideas of childhood and the education of children. In the eighteenth century, the most important names were Watts and Wesley, John Wesley being the greatest individual social force of the century, and Charles Wesley being the finest hymn writer of any century and himself a great force acting upon society. If the large contribution of Isaac Watts must be reduced to few words, it can be said that he joined Locke's tolerance with exalted Puritanism. Charles Wesley joined High Church doctrine with a great sense of social mission and a great knowledge of life. Literature written especially for children may almost be said to have come into existence in the Augustan Age. The English hymn as a literary form may almost be said to have come into being with the lyrics of Watts. Though Watts and Wesley had much in common, Wesley's view of child life and his poetic method both are different from Watts's.[5] As man and as poet, Wesley's

---

[4] On the subject of these historical developments, see Erik Routley, *The English Carol* (London 1958) 117–140; Percy Scholes, *The Puritans and Music* (New York 1934); Harvey Darton, *Children's Books in England* (London 1932), 53–69; Cornelia Meigs, et al, *A Critical History of Children's Literature* (New York 1953), especially p 58–60 on Locke.

[5] There is a doctrinal difference between Wesley's picture of the Holy Child and Watts's opening poem in *Horae Lyricae* in his section of Sacred Love, "The Hazard of Loving the Creatures."

Nature has soft but powerful bands,
  And Reason she controls;
While children with their little hands
  Hang closest to our souls.

Thoughtless they act the old serpent's part;
  What tempting things they be!
Lord, how they twine about our heart,
  And draw it off from Thee!

Dear Sovereign, break these fetters off . . .

confidence was in the power of myth to act upon the imagination, and thus to educate, to accomplish didactic, exemplary, and energizing functions in mind and heart and life. He vivified medieval ideas in terms of eighteenth-century realism, uniting a sacramental sense of the beauty of holiness with strenuous evangelicism.

Wesley, like Blake, spoke his whole mind to a child, and his entire view of life is present in his children's songs. The holy child lives in a pastoral world that has its unity in the Lamb, and all the rich equivalences of that heroic figure are established. Care and skill bestow a common life and a common image upon God and Man, yet leave the doctrine unmarred by blasphemy, so great is his reverence for life and for the Source of life. The child is both holy and heroic. Angels attend him. Lamb and child are beautiful by their very names. Children's voices blend naturally with the songs of the heavenly hosts. The child is "Part of God's family," and decidedly the best part. Wesley's audacity taught every child to sing that he was in person "God's favorite child," but they sang in chorus, aware that it was no secret or exclusive favoritism. The Lamb was not nursery equipment to be outgrown. At any age the heart might gambol as to the tabor's sound. Joy in the Lamb was a responsive joy called forth in answer to external reality. This is not a children's hymn:

> In the heavenly Lamb
> Thrice happy I am,
> And my heart it doth dance at the sound of His name. (v 24)

The ideal was that the child should live always within the man, who, while growing "strong in grace" as the years passed, should live in innocency of spirit. With regard to that quality, "Let us be children still." On earth, men pronounce judgments upon themselves by hourly choices between love and cruelty toward those who have no defense against cruelty. The Lamb will pronounce the final sum of these judgments upon men and nations. In that sense, the Lamb was the sign of the child, and in this aspect of his nature, the child is Judge of man and of society.

As in the Hebraic imagination, Wesley also accomplished a fusion of daily life with the entire myth of the Lamb. There seemed to him to be a natural union between the life of a child and Psalm 23, Isaiah 40, the incidents when Jesus held a child in His arms (Matt. 18: 1–11; 19: 13–15; Luke 8: 16–17), the parable of the ninety and nine, the account of the New Birth (John 3) and the New Jerusalem. Often one is reminded of those two figures of speech in which the Wesleys described their own conversion experiences, the heart strangely warmed, the arms held out in love.[6]

Blake's songs were written in that area where the hymn, the pastoral, and children's literature unite. The songs are not hymns, in the strict meaning of songs intended for congregational singing. Neither were the children's books by Bunyan, Watts, or Mrs Barbauld, although all three had some relation to the hymn form. Let us defer for the moment the question of what may have been Blake's relation to these three forms of writing and his attitude toward them; whatever the attitude may have been, Charles Wesley was his closest predecessor.

Blake's entire book is pastoral, and his pastoral world is centered in the Lamb. Nine of the *Songs of Innocence* speak of lamb, sheep, and shepherd. Child, lamb, and the Christ Child are closely related. The child is associated with angels and the songs of the heavenly hosts. In his helpless state, the child is the judge of society. The sufferings of the Lamb in the state of Inno-

[6] To little ones, and not to men,
　　Is grace and glory given;
　Children they must become again,
　　Or never enter heaven. (vi 453)

Surrounded by a flaming host
　Of bright cherubic powers,
Not all the kings of heaven can boast
　Of such a guard as ours.
　　(vi 448; cf II Kings 6:16–17)

Loving Jesus, gentle Lamb,
　In Thy gracious hands I am;
Make me, Saviour, what Thou art;
　Live Thyself within my heart.

I shall then show forth Thy praise,
　Serve Thee all my happy days:
Then the world shall always see
　Christ, the Holy Child, in me. (vi 442)

Still, as we grow in years, in grace
　And wisdom let us grow;
But never leave Thy dear embrace,
　And never evil know.

Strong let us in Thy grace abide,
　But ignorant of ill;
In malice, subtlety and pride,
　Let us be children still. (vi 449)

Glory to God, and praise, and power,
　Honour and thanks be given;
Children and cherubim adore
　The Lord of earth and heaven. (vi 446)

Train up Thy hardy soldiers, Lord,
　In all their Captain's steps to tread!
Or send them to proclaim Thy word,
　Thy gospel through the world to spread,
Freely as they received to give,
　And preach the death by which they live.
　　(vi 409)

Dangers and snares abound,
　And ever close us round;
Numberless malicious powers
　Fight against us night and day;
Satan as a lion roars,
　Watching to devour his prey. (vi 398)

The unsuspicious stranger
To our malignant race
From every hidden danger
Deliver by Thy grace.
From popular infection,
From every great offense,
Thy love be the protection
Of thoughtless innocence. (vii 131)

Wesley made Psalm 117 into a lullaby for a sick baby, and a prayer for those who watch beside sick-beds.

Sleep, that soothingly restores
Weary nature's wasted powers,
Gift of an indulgent God,
Be it on our child bestowed. (vii 128)

cence are both patent and latent. The chimney sweeper, the little lost boy, the emmet and her children, the little black boy are in danger. The robin, the mother, the baby, the Maker all weep. Wolves and tigers howl for prey, and angels and parents may be powerless to protect. Tears and woe are the burden of the last song. In Experience, sheep have threatening horns. Worms fly like dragons. Deadly apples grow on trees in a garden. One may betray one's own angel. Parents may betray a child. The City is marred by plagues (from which the blood of the Lamb should protect the first-born), usury (sign of a failure of social conscience), desecrated churches, defiled rivers and streets. The two contrary states interpenetrate and interact upon one another, as may be seen from the four songs placed first in one section of the book and then in the other, appropriate to either section depending on relative emphasis upon elements present in both sections. In Experience, there are echoes of the pastoral passages from Isaiah, where lion and lamb are at peace, and both sections are rich in allusions to Job, Revelation, the Psalms, the Crucifixion, the Lord's Prayer, the wren that will not fall unmarked, the cattle upon a thousand hills. In both states there are city and country, joy and sorrow, danger and injustice, bewilderment, depriva-tion, and mercy. And in both states, the child is holy.

When the development of hymn meters is seen in historical sequence, it is apparent that Blake is closer to Wesley than to any other poet. Wesley's virtuosity in the lyric form has challenged the attention of scholars and musicians, and intensive studies of his modulations are available. Frank Baker has accumulated this work, and far superseded it by his own work. It is Dr Baker's opinion that no eighteenth-century poet can be compared to Wesley in inventiveness and mastery of the lyric form, and of the nineteenth-century poets, Shelley alone is comparable.[7] No such exhaustive studies have been made of Blake's metrics,[8] but his use of meter was strong and subtle and throughout his career he experimented boldly in verse forms. He experiments in his children's songs, but he shares Wesley's stanza forms, rhyme words, variation of measure and tone, and subtle repetition of sound. Little is known of Blake's acquaintance with music and the theatre. *A Book for a Rainy Day* (London 1845) by John Thomas Smith is source of the statement that Blake sang his own early songs. My main source of information about "Blake's

---

[7] Frank Baker, *Representative Verse of Charles Wesley* (London 1962) p xliv. Dr Baker's work on metrics is outstanding, and he had made noteworthy contributions in every problem of Wesleyan hymnody. His bibliographical information supplements that given in Richard Green's *Wesley Bibliography*. See p 139–140 for his dating of the children's hymns.

[8] Miss Alicia Ostriker makes a brave beginning on the metrics in *Vision and Verse in William Blake* (Madison and Milwaukee 1965). — D.V.E.

relation to music" is the composers who set his words and the singers who perform the songs, Philip Bezansen, who has set them for David Lloyd, Henry Cowell, who has set them for Theodor Uppman and Roland Hayes. "What is the text asking for?" is their one concern, and the answer includes details of orchestration and all musical elements. *Songs of Innocence* asks for a powerful male voice. Arguments of similarities between two poets' verse forms are not convincing without mathematical proof and exclusion of other possible influences, but I will offer a single example of what may be a specific connection between the poets. For all who know Wesley poetry, "The Shepherd," Blake's second song, has a Wesley tune.[9]

Studies of Blake's theology and philosophy have included some references to John Wesley.[10] Jacob Bronowski has written of Blake's relation to the evangelical movement and its hymns.[11] Students of Wesley have seen in

[9] The history of the tune shows that Blake could have picked it up in Vauxhall, in the theatre, on the streets, or in slightly altered form from John Newton's hymn, "How tedious and tasteless the hours," a type of pastoral lament. The early American folk tune to which Newton's words are sung in America will accommodate Wesley's "Lucy" songs, but Wesley's need more dramatic music. The tune, "Lucy," was written by Dr John Worgan, organist for four or five famous churches, who played and composed also for the public gardens. "Lucy" was written for Vauxhall. A shepherdess sings to her dead lover and longs to join him in the grave. The words by Moore begin, "Hark! Hark! 'tis a voice from the tomb." Even in Vauxhall the song was a pastoral *liebestod*. Wesley used it for many shepherd songs. "Thou Shepherd of Israel" from his cycle (IX 362–366) based on the Song of Solomon is quoted later. He used it for those funeral hymns of his which are the soul's response to the summons of the Shepherd-Bridegroom, "Rise up, my love, my fair one, and come away." If it had these associations for Blake, the stanza form adds to the note of pastoral lament and death that has been noted in the *Songs of Innocence*. Wesley wrote about 10,000 lines of anapestic or mixed iambic and anapestic verse. The remarkable effect of dignity and emotional force won by him from the "vulgar anapests" is credited as one of his metrical triumphs. See James T. Lightwood, *Hymn Tunes and Their Story* (1905) 137–138; Maurice Frost, "The Tunes Associated with Hymn Singing in the Lifetime of the Wesleys," *Hymn Society of Great Britain and Ireland Bulletin* IV no 8 (Winter 1957/8) p 117–126; "Worgan, John," Grove's *Dictionary of Music*. I am indebted to Austin Lovelace, who has made available to me in conversations some of his fathomless knowledge of hymn music, and to correspondence with Carlton Young; Dr Lovelace and Dr Young are the editors of the forthcoming edition of the *Methodist Hymnal*.

[10] John G. Davis, *The Theology of William Blake* (Oxford 1948), and Denis Saurat, *Blake and Modern Thought* (New York 1964), speak briefly of John Wesley, and conclude correctly that he and Blake were Protestants; they give neither Wesley nor Blake credit for much originality of thought.

[11] J. Bronowski, *A Man Without a Mask* (London 1947) 111 *et passim*, considers within the context of social history Blake's relation to the evangelical movement and makes valuable and stimulating comparison between his diction and that of the evangelical hymns. This material is reprinted in *William Blake and the Age of Revolution* (New York 1965) 143 *et passim*. His comment on Wesley hymns quotes John Wesley three times, the hymn chosen for comparison being the fairly literal translation of Tersteegen's "Verborgne Gottes liebe du." Charles Wesley's *Wrestling Jacob* is described by an enthymeme which leaves me unsure as to what major premise has been omitted: "We should think Charles Wesley's Wrestling Jacob a blasphemous poem." If this means, "I think it blasphemous," it is an interesting parallel to Manning's opinion of this poem and "Thou Shepherd of Israel," that nothing short of divine inspiration keeps the daring emotion sane and reverent and orthodox. Manning says it is an extreme example of Wesley's

Blake's writings his use of Methodist vocabulary and ideas.[12] Some studies
have been made of Blake's possible knowledge and use of children's books
by Bunyan,[13] Watts,[14] and Mrs Barbauld,[15] of which use there is internal

---

audacity. Unlike Bronowski, he does postulate divine inspiration, and does not think the poem
blasphemous.

[12] The most discreet discussion of Blake's "Methodist" vocabulary is by Frederick C. Gill, *The
Romantic Movement and Methodism* (London 1937) 146–159. Thomas B. Shepherd, *Methodism
and the Literature of the Eighteenth Century* (London 1940), cites Gill and adds his own statement (the only such statement known to me) that Blake's songs for children appear to have been
influenced by Charles Wesley more than by any other writer. Robert F. Gleckner, "Blake and
Wesley," *Notes and Queries*, III (1956) 522–524, assumes that John Wesley, not Charles, wrote
the hymns for the Kingswood scholars, and argues that Blake satirized the hymns in "Holy
Thursday." Frank Baker (143–145) ascribes the hymns to Charles Wesley; but John Wesley's
authorship is not considered an impossibility, his collaboration is also a possibility, and his
influence is a certainty. If Blake parodied Wesley, then his children's songs did begin in some
relation to Wesley, for this is the first, the supposed "parody" of Mrs Barbauld the second
(453) of the songs in *An Island in the Moon*. If Blake originally meant the song as satire of
Wesley's "hypocrisy" (and this is Mr Gleckner's statement), he altered his attitude at some
time, either before or after he published *Songs of Innocence*. "To the Deists"(199) refutes this
old charge of hypocrisy, both as regards Methodists in general, and specifically by name with
reference to the founder of Kingswood School, Whitefield.

[13] John Bunyan's last book, *A Book for Boys and Girls: or Country Rhymes for Children* (1686),
was edited by E. S. Buchanan (American Tract Society 1928). There was a second edition in
1701 titled *A Book for Boys and Girls: or Temporal Things Spiritualized*, which reduced the
number of emblems from 74 to 49. In the ninth edition (1724) and subsequently it was called
Divine Emblems: or Temporal Things Spiritualized, with cuts, and many alterations in the text.
The book is not widely known, and the American Tract edition is out of print and unobtainable;
Julian's *Dictionary of Hymmnology* reports its existence only by hearsay. Rosemary Freeman,
English Emblem Books (London 1948) 204–228, gives an excellent study of it, and Darton,
loc. cit., comments on it. Any conjecture about Blake's possible feelings about the book would
depend greatly, I think, on which edition we are assuming he saw. Vivian de Sola Pinto assumes
antipathy, but the original work has much in it that might have delighted Blake, chiefly the
manner of addressing animals as kinsmen and the combination of mysticism with rough good
humor. "Of the Spouse of Christ" is a pastoral poem befitting country rhymes.

> Who's this, that cometh from the wilderness,
> Like smoky pillars, thus perfumed with myrrh?
>
>   . . .
>
> Well, lady, well, God hath been good to thee;
> Thou of an outcast now art made a queen.
> Few or none may with thee compared be,
> A beggar made thus high is seldom seen.
> Take heed of pride.

   Bunyan wanted the child to fear hell, but nothing in the natural world, and he jokes with
the child about fear of animals.

> What! What! A human creature and afraid
> Of frogs, dogs, cats, rats, mice, or such-like cr'atur'?

In friendly jest, he speaks to the lark "Thou simple bird!" and to the cuckoo, "Thou booby,
say'st thou nothing but *Cuckoo*? Well, thou hast fellows!" Recognizing a child's natural affinity
with pigs, he gives them a delightfully haughty fatted swine.

> Ah, Sirrah! I perceive thou art corn-fed.
> But Hog, why look'st so big? Why dost so flounce?
> Why snort and fling away?

evidence only. No investigation has been made of Blake's possible acquaintance with the children's hymns and psalm versions of Christopher Smart.

Why indeed? It would be many a year before an English poet would address you again in this man-to-man fashion. There is a beautiful snail, emblem of those who seek Christ, and have their journey shortened by God's grace and their natural food given on the journey by God's hand, so that they come at last to what they seek, and their reward matches their striving, not their strength. It has a lovely sound.

> She goes but slowly, but she goeth sure,
> She stumbles not, as stronger Creatures do:
> Her Journey's shorter, so she may endure
> Better than they which do much further go.
>   She makes no noise, but stilly seizeth on
> The Flower or Herb appointed for her food
> The which she quietly doth feed upon,
> While others range, and gare, and find no good.
>   And tho' she doth but very softly go,
> However, 'tis not fast, nor slow, but sure;
> And certainly they that do travel so,
> The prize they do aim at, they do procure.

[14] It is assumed by most critics that Blake knew Watts's *Divine and Moral Songs*, that the two cradle songs stand in some relation to each other, that Blake would have been offended by Watts's Calvinism, but might have enjoyed the poems, as he enjoyed the Calvinist Cowper. See Vivian de Sola Pinto, "William Blake, Isaac Watts and Mrs Barbauld," *The Divine Vision* (London 1957) 65–89, where Bunyan is also discussed; and "Isaac Watts and the Adventurous Muse," *English Association Essays and Studies*, no 20 (1934) 86–108. As contrast to Blake's anapests, I call attention to Watts in merry mood, as he celebrates one of his great loves, the sky of England.

> How fine has the day been! how bright was the sun,
> How lovely and joyful the course he has run!
> Though he rose in a mist when his race he begun
>   And there followed some droppings of rain;
> But now the fair traveller's come to the west,
> His rays are all gold, and his beauties are best;
> He paints the sky gay as he sinks to his rest,
>   And foretells a bright rising again.

Watts, like Mrs Barbauld, wrote under the influence of Blake's chosen enemies, in this case, Calvin and Locke. His lines are full of moralistic injunctions, but there is in him much that is both kindly and charming.

[15] Anna Letitia Aiken Barbauld (1743–1825) was sister of Dr John Aiken and wife of the Reverend Rochemont Barbauld, both members of the faculty of Warrington Academy. At the request of William Enfield of Warrington, she began writing hymns in 1772 and wrote till her death in 1825. She taught with her husband and brother, and was highly respected as teacher, poet, educational theorist, and hymn writer. She was devoutly Unitarian and contentiously Rousseauistic, having learned from her husband, who was of French extraction, a great admiration for Rousseau's *Emile*. It is assumed that Blake met her at the home of the Mathews, and it is assumed that he knew her work. Its relation to Blake's *Songs* has been variously assessed, Vivian de Sola Pinto seeing her as "the last link" between Blake and the tradition of children's literature, and E. D. Hirsch, *Innocence and Experience* (New Haven 1964), placing great stress upon Blake's sympathy for her and the influence of her *Hymns in Prose for Children* (1782). The images cited as borrowed from her are Scriptural images and appear in the usual Scriptural sequences and associations; both her "hymns" and her other books for children are in prose. She seems to me tactless; the child has no privacy and no more real freedom than Emile. The child is in no danger except those that threaten the inhabitants of *An Island in the Moon*: being talked to death or bored to death by her personae who endlessly explain the obvious. Grown people (who buy children's books) still like her and always did; I have seen a 57th edition (1864) of her prose hymns.

Certainly this acquaintance is highly probable, and internal evidence seems
to show the work nearer in mood and structure to Smart's than to any writer
other than Wesley.[16]

Recent comment by literary critics, theologians, and sociologists has made
an effort to disassociate Blake from all three of the genres, children's literature, hymn, and pastoral; various degrees of satire, self-satire, parody, paradox, and irony have been announced as present in the songs. The three genres
are notoriously sensitive areas for critics, reactions being governed by individual tempers and the temper of the times. The three forms were not in vogue
with the intelligentsia during the eighteenth century, enjoyed a noticeable
rise in status in the nineteenth century, and are again under a cloud. Efforts
have been made to clear Blake's name by separating him from all three.
During the nineteenth century in this pastoral scene there coagulated a
syrupy pool of self-worship disguised as pastoral nostalgia, and the landscape became densely populated with cardboard shepherds and stuffed
replicas of mama's little lamb. Blake's image did become flecked with this
syrup, and some critics now are cleaning away the smears. It may not be
necessary, however, to throw out the baby with the bath. I think the songs

[16] Christopher Smart, *Hymns for the Amusement of Children* (1770), in *Collected Poems*, ed
Norman Callan, 2 vols (London 1949) II 963–1001. The word amusement does not suggest
frivolity; Watts wrote all his songs, hymns, and psalm versions for the amusement and entertain-
ment of his readers. As Blake might have been pleased with Cowper's love of animals, as he was
excited by Wordsworth's May festival, so he may have liked Smart's "Mirth in May," where
birds, children, lambs, colts, horses, dogs, silkworms, and dormice rejoice together in sweet
musical verse (II 991), and may have liked Smart's insistence on how seriously the King of
Kings regarded animals. Smart's psalm versions have lovely pastoral passages.

> Great today thy song and rapture
> In the choir of Christ and Wren.
>
>   . . .
>
> Spinks and ouzels sing sublimely,
> "We too have a Saviour born";
> Whiter blossoms burst untimely
> On the blest Mosaic thorn.
>
>   . . .
>
> God all-bounteous, all-creative,
> Whom no ills from good dissuade,
> Is incarnate, and a native
> Of the very world he made. (II 847)

William Hayley, Cowper's friend and biographer, discussed with the Reverend Thomas
Carwardine the manuscript of *Jubilate Agno*, part of the Carwardine family papers. Hayley may
have called to Blake's attention Smart's other writings, or Blake may have interested himself in
this celebrated case of poetic madness at a date early enough to make possible some influence
of Smart's work on his songs for children. Smart's work, like Wesley's and Blake's, is a union
of hymn, pastoral, and children's literature.

are children's literature, pastorals, and are related to the hymn tradition, but I say it without animus, and am indebted to some writers whose critical bias and past experiences have led them to the opposite conclusion. Most critics who find the songs "sardonic" in tone have done Blake the courtesy of removing them from the area of children's literature, saying that he did not intend them for children. This opinion takes from Blake the praise of having worked with outstanding success in a very difficult genre; but to read the book thus and classify it as children's literature removes Blake himself from decency of manners. If proof should be found that Blake was satirizing children's literature in general, or specifically the little Watts-baby in his cradle, Bunyan's little puritan watching the ant for moral lessons, Mrs Barbauld's little Emile of Warrington, Wesley's lamb-child in Innocence, or Wesley's busy little Methodist in existential Experience, I should not be shattered by the news, though it would cause me to distrust my ear for song, and, as things now stand, it would be news to me. If it should be proved that Blake sang the song of Moses and the Lamb only in tones of ironic paradox, I should remind myself that Moses was something of an ironist and the Lamb was capable of paradox. Wits and parodists have been found within the fold, and satirists have been canonized. If Blake admired John Wesley and yet thought the hymn movement silly, he was in the excellent company of Samuel Wesley, the older brother, and Dr Samuel Johnson. If he decided, immediately after the death of Charles Wesley, to issue a book correcting those points upon which they did not agree, as he did for Milton, then the book could be read as corrigenda, not even then, I think, as satire. His *Milton* is not satire. In sum, although I hear no satiric tone at all, I insist upon only two things. Blake did not address *children* in veiled and sardonic satire. Second, if he is satirizing a literary form or a system of thought, his target seems to have been Charles Wesley.

The earliest songs of which we have record were set in a framework of satire. They appear in *An Island in the Moon,* a more mundane lunar landscape than Milton's, or Pope's satire of Milton's in *The Rape of the Lock,* or Swift's suggestion of such an island. It is a half-way house between Laputa and Crotchet Castle, much in the mood of Samuel Foote's stage impromptus, ridiculing many of Foote's objects of satire, one of which was the enthusiastic preacher. It is peopled with eccentrics through whose eccentricities Blake satirizes amateur science, soirees, bluestockings, children's songs, and various types of enthusiasm.

The songs which appear in *Songs of Innocence* turned out to be not as good jokes as he had intended and better songs than he had at first suspected. He left *An Island in the Moon* in manuscript, and profited by his successes with the songs when he decided to write for children. (Later, in 1791, he was at work on the illustrations for Mary Wollstonecraft's *Original Stories,* and by 1793 had produced his own work, *For Children: The Gates of Paradise.*) The songs altered in two respects; the framework changed and the audience changed. Change of audience may alter tone, and this is egregiously true where a child is the audience. The framing of a piece of writing affects its tone. Faulkner's Easter sermon in *The Sound and the Fury* might be parody without its framing and the audience to which it is addressed. Given that setting, the sermon generates tragic emotion. Addressed to the uncorrupted innocence of Dilsey, the sermon cannot be satire, and that statement would hold if Faulkner had written it originally for a minstrel show. The words Aloysha speaks to the Child in Experience in the epilogue of *The Brothers Karamazov* have not satisfied all critics. The epilogue and the Easter sermon are good writing or bad writing, as you please to find them; you may feel that the authors erred in allowing these two terrible novels to find their rest in such words. Poor writing both may be, but what the passages cannot be, given that audience and setting, is satiric. Dostoievsky meant every namby-pamby word. So, I think, did Blake, and I think the songs are perhaps his best work, an important part of his remarkably consistent canon.

Blake decided to alter his book for children, *The Gates of Paradise*; when he did, he properly indicated his change of audience, and labeled the altered work *For the Sexes* (734). But every copy of *Songs of Innocence and of Experience* is covered by the opening statement that "Every child might joy to hear" the songs, and he never produced the second section apart from it.[16a] Since the entire book is his own careful work, the statement cannot be an oversight or a typographical error. He said he did not write for idiots, and said in the same letter that not all children were idiots, and that he was happy to know that children could "elucidate" his visions and had "taken greater delight in contemplating my Pictures than I ever hoped" (677). Certainly the book seems to be addressed to children, not giving them all their tiny minds could hold, but giving them all he had to give. All of Blake is in it. As his amazing imagination summoned his prophetic forebears, so by that imagination he speaks to his future, speaks sweetly and seriously to those who in time will inherit his riches and his tasks. Children like it when they hear it. They ask no questions. They know what happened to Oona. They

[16a] See note on page 148, below.

will repeat the sweet sounds as if they understood "Calling the lapsed soul," but they neither question it nor describe it.

Description pays slight compliment to those rare writings that offer the holy child his own portrait drawn with tact, without sentimentality or nostalgia. Description cannot convey the pure singing voice, the power of direct address, the ability to speak to and for the child, the good manners that can enter a child's world without being offensive or nosy. Someone should have risked arrest in order to send J. R. R. Tolkien his best critical review. It appeared anonymously, scrawled on a placard in a New York subway: "Frodo was here." Such books — Wesley's and Blake's and Mr Tolkien's — will make their own way in the world. Where imagination listens, they create their audience, and confer both innocence and experience upon it. Where imagination is absent, they are helpless and meaningless. They are able to caution the future, able to say without self-consciousness or self-righteousness, "Unless a halfling, of his own free and difficult choice, relinquishes that Mystery which blurs and makes him invisible, the dark may come, man's tyranny over man, and your world may become a furnace, a mill, with impersonal cruelty for its only moving force."

Differ as they do about details of what the Good may be, the apocalyptic visions agree in this: He that sitteth upon the throne is able to make all things new. The Good is fresh; it is evil that is stale. They tell of the ever-changing and unboring modes of the Good. They tell of evil, but are never so tactless as to speak of the worst possible evil, that a child may become, not a chimney sweeper, but master of chimney sweepers. At no age is success measured by the number of chimney sweepers one can boss around. (Rare in children's books.) Being men, not women, they cannot ask directly for what they want most from the child: Stay with me. Two of the three are on the side of the Establishment, but something keeps all three from being what the Elect call really moral, sensible, high-principled men. They calmly make insufferable demands on the imagination. They pander to natural love of thrills. They are overly confiding in myth and metaphor. They do not mortify human pride with statistics. They contrive to make children important in their own eyes, and their books need to be off-set by many books that will mortify that pride by persuading a child he really wants to read, "Hop. Hop. I can hop." They say it is a tough world, and their books need to be undermined by many books telling of a world that is more comfy. They tend to make the Elect uneasy; they are not quite content with the *status quo,* not persuaded there is no further need for quests, a change of heart, mental fight. They are not realistic,

for no one can draw the holy child from model. The artist perceives the
Presences known to passion, piety, and affection, living in their own myths,
and tact establishes the relation between myth and life. Abstraction will not
accomplish the results; theories do not account for such books. Blake did
indeed have a theory about contraries, and it is fully set forth in this book.
Wesley had a theory — based on I know not what evidence — that there
was in the time of Primitive Christianity no such artificial division between
child and man as the modern world knows. Mr Tolkien has theories about
linguistics, but they do not account for his way of naming things as if he were
creating the world.

Bunyan, Watts, and Mrs Barbauld abound in moralistic injunctions. They
begin with a firm idea of general moral truth and lay down the law (a kind
and reasonable law stated with various degrees of good humor) in a closed
system of logic. Wesley also abounds in moralistic injunctions, and asks of
the child a much more rigorous life than these writers; but his songs open out
on a world where some tremendous experience is going to take place. The
sole grounds for discipline, for voluntary participation in discipline, are the
demands of that experience.

Watts and Bunyan want all fear concentrated in fear of hell and dismiss
any fear of the natural world. Smart's songs give a pre-romantic feeling of
being at home in nature. Mrs Barbauld was completely at one with the world,
and a dull, safe world it is. "If you fall, little lambs, you will not be hurt; there
is spread under you a carpet of soft grass; it is spread on purpose to receive
you." Certainly Blake offered his little lambs no such bland and Rouseauistic
picture of life.[17] Certainly Wesley did not.

Touch the fabric of a child's life at any point, and it trembled under the
hand with joy and awe and pain. The sum of human passion entered into the
beginnings of life. There is no parallel in hymnody (there are few in literature) for Wesley's hymn cycle that describes childbirth from the onset of
labor to delivery. When his first child was born, he sat beside his wife while
she sank into death and was restored by what he thought was a miracle. Her
fear of death was on him. The reality of her screams and sweat and dreadful

[17] David V. Erdman, *Blake: Prophet Against Empire* (Princeton 1954) 113, 116, says the
songs began in "good-natured" satire of Mrs Barbauld, that the element of danger is Blake's
addition to the picture of life as given in her "hymns," that the songs as they stand in *Songs of
Innocence* are not satiric in tone. Although I cannot hear Blake's songs as having much (or any)
real relation to her work, I can see that Mrs Nannicantipot may have had Mrs Barbauld for a
prototype, and I nourish a suspicion that his picture of the character may have been not completely good-natured. Blake's idea that a talkative woman is a cage for a man's imagination may
have begun in those bluestocking soirees.

weakness was before him as her mangled body lapsed into unconsciousness and waked again and again to new pain. The hymns are as decorous in language as they are harrowing in their accurate reporting of symptoms.[18]

The baby lived and was, of course, named John. The father doted on the pretty little boy and his songs move to the frisking of his "giddy child." When he was sixteen months old, the child died of smallpox. The father's lifelong grief took many forms in his prayers and meditations. Birth and death seemed in every way so close. His funeral hymns sound like Christmas carols with their reiterated line, "Angels, rejoice! a child is born!" *Puer natus est* became for him a gospel of joy fraught with pain. At times it seemed almost as if Jackie slept with Sammy and little Charles and little Sally, the four together, deep in the mystery of sleep.

> The arms within whose soft embrace
>   My sleeping babes I see
> They comprehend unbounded space
>   And grasp infinity. (xi 32)

But he dismissed morbid thoughts to sing of games and the tea table, vacation in the country, the heat and weariness of moving day, the embarrassment of losing his job, the wrench of sending his little girl away to boarding school. He was afraid of spoiling his children and tried to be firm with them, wondering if he were more wicked or more ridiculous in acting like a "lion" or an "eastern potentate" around the house. He sang of children limp from fever, teething, dizzy from whirling round in their play, beautiful in their naughtiness that was almost indistinquishable from their "thoughtless innocence." Many students of Wesley, among them his editor Osborn, have thought *Family Hymns* his crowning achievement. His days were full of every problem of the education and welfare of his own children, including the special problem of rearing two child prodigies, for his two sons were musical geniuses. His home had a stream of visitors bringing problems from every walk of life. The burden of children's problems fell on him and his brother in the congregations of their far ridings. His lambs were his own

---

[18] See Osborn vii 49–72, 141–146.

Jesu, Son of Mary, hear
   Our help-imploring cry;
Lord of life and death, appear
   With Thy salvation nigh:
God of grace and endless power,
And never-failing faithfulness,
   Bring her through her torturing hour,
      And bid her live in peace.

. . .

By the travails of Thy soul,
   Thy more than mortal pain,
All her fear of death control,
   Her fainting heart sustain:
Streams of consolation shower
On one Thy love delights to bless,
   Bring her through her torturing hour,
      And bid her live in peace. (vii 142)

babies, and those of the brutal, the insane, the drunken, the vain, the silly, the evil-tempered.

Wesley's Child, like Blake's, is holy both in Innocence and in Experience, but there is an important difference in the states of Experience as described by the two poets. In every instance, Blake's Child is a passive sufferer and has no part in his own fate, no control over circumstances. Wesley commits the Child's fate into the Child's own hands under God, and the Child is the Church in essence, with every office, privilege, and duty his *in esse* or *in posse*. The Wesley Child in Innocence is a lively revivification of the Holy Child; in Experience, he takes the shape of another medieval figure, the knight errant, and again, every event of real life takes its true reality from being subsumed in myth. This is a busy, bustling little Methodist, as real as Tom Jones, but angels are his squires. The very school curriculum is a "ten-year siege," and the comitatus is vowed to the assault. The young valiants walk in "secret paths," and have need of "other eyes / Than flesh and blood supplies" to find out the perilous path. As by enchantment, "Mountains, alas! on mountains rise" to bar them from the envisioned goal, news of which had come to them by prophets and seers. A fearsome world, but through it blew winds of unearthly fragrance and strains of unearthly song that harmonized with their own singing. Tokens were everywhere. Fire and fountain, earth and air, this flowery carpet, every tree told of warning or comfort to the doughty ones who could read the markings. There were deeds of derring-do, impossible tasks, inevitable defeats, and victory assured. Above was a great cloud of witnesses and there was goodly company on the road. The way was hazardous, but the waybread was given. None of this goodly company is in Blake's world. Nothing is to be gained there by any Fellowship or Meeting. It is a lonely world. Only the artist can act for good; but so long as child and artist are in touch, each has a sort of safety and hope in the other.

Biographical information has special importance in the reading of Wesley and Blake — not that they are important for being directly autobiographical. Neither poet tells precisely what is going on in ordinary life; neither poet recounts the stories from the Bible. From both sources, life and the myth with which life is fused, there is felt the driving force of some series of events in cause-and-effect relationship, the movement of some plot that is evoked but often remains an untold story. Between the myth and the Bible there often will intervene another story, but this story is never used as allegory; it rather is part of the myth which has been absorbed into the Bible according to a mode of thought that is quite different from Bunyan's or Spenser's use of allegory. Two hundred years of explication have aligned events in Wesley's

Blake, *Songs of Innocence* 1789, Illuminated Printing
(Berg Collection, The New York Public Library)

First page of "Spring" in Blake's illuminated printing of *Songs of Innocence* (Berg Collection, The New York Public Library)

life with particular hymns and have located the sources of his allusions to extra-Biblical material; books are being published in increasing numbers to stand with the already existing libraries of Wesleyana. Explication of Blake's double plot-line is in progress, accelerated by the acknowledgement of most scholars that his poetry was written by a sane and efficient Cockney who had a keen eye on the world around him even while he dined with Isaiah. Scholars locate analogues for what appear to be neoplatonic stories, Indian creation legends, astrological romances, theories of evolution, exotic fables, and hermetic fictions that combine with his myth as Wesley absorbed fictions and philosophies into his. Other scholars ascertain those current events that shaped Blake's poems by way of his daily life. Few scholars claim such gratitude as Blake's explicators.[19] Few poets have had their reading public so expanded by their explicators. Blake's obscurity alone does not account for this gratitude. Even in his simplest lyric, Blake is telling some story, never merely making an assertion or establishing a mood. Even when his moods are perceptible and his assertions are discernible, the mind is teased by that not-quite-told narrative that drives the poem along. One wants to know the story as well as to feel that there is a story somewhere in the undercurrent. When this method works, it is great, but the method can result in bad poetry — confusing, opaque, misleading, bombastic. When the poetry is fully understood, it may appear to be quite the reverse — meek as Moses and clear as day; but still, that is bad poetry.

All who read Wesley mark his "extraordinary fusion, in his imagination, of his own life with the life of the New Testament." The quality has been praised by Norman Nicholson (whom I quote), Bernard Manning, and Donald Davie.[20] Both the sophistication of Wesley's art and the "divine audacity" of his thought have to do with the total fusion of life and myth. If one knows the stories to which he alludes and their place in the continuing and continuous story of revelation, one is in better position to talk about sophistication and audacity; but when the poetry is successful, the entire effect is available to any imaginative audience, and that "field of force" makes itself felt without detailed knowledge of the myth from whence it comes. But it is not always successful. An example may be made of Wesley's

[19] My own debts are many. First, to Sir Geoffrey Keynes. To David Erdman. To Northrop Frye, his work on Blake, his work in critical theory, and his making available to the public Peter Fisher's *The Valley of Vision* (Toronto 1961). To Kathleen Raine, her astuteness in the public domain and her generosity in making time for talk. To scholars who, like Harold Bloom and S. Foster Damon make Blake studies a university composed of many schools of thought.

[20] Bernard Lord Manning, *The Hymns of Wesley and Watts* (London 1942). Norman Nicholson, "Wesley and Watts," *TLS* (Aug 6 1954) xliv-xlv. Donald Davie, *Purity of Diction in English Verse* (Oxford 1953) 72–73.

writings on the prophet Samuel. They never quite jell. Some of Blake's work has this annoying viscosity. The total interpretation of Samuel, picked up from all Wesley's writings, is so marked with grandeur and compassion that it deserves the name of high tragedy, or would if he had ever actually written it. I would say the same of Blake's tragedy of Moses and Aaron; one picks up the gist *passim,* but cannot help wishing he had written it.[21]

The story of Samuel records that Hannah "gave her son suck," and this statement caused Wesley to burst out:

> Not like the mothers of our day
> Who of all care themselves divest
> And thrust their new-born babe away
> And hang it on another's breast. (ix 149)

That is vulgar. It was no business of his who employed a wet nurse. Even this nadir is not idle railing, nor is it, as it appears to be, a declaration of a moral law for mothers. Nine children were born to the Wesleys. The mother was able to nurse three, and they lived. The others died. A general moral law would imply that his wife was on the wrong side of that law, and certainly no blame devolved on her. Some extra-logical logic had formed an association in his mind between this giving of life and life itself, between the withholding of this source of life and the death of the child.

The very name Samuel was a sign of mercy and law moving down from generation to generation, from unknowing to knowing. It was the name of

---

21 The proper example from Blake's work is Job, but I am not sure I understand how Blake interpreted Job. The principle upon which he selected and located the texts in his illustrations of the Book of Job is not clear to me. But his interpretation of Moses and Aaron has been brilliantly expounded by Mr Frye from a mythopoeic point of view and by Mr Fisher from an existential point of view. I am not happy with anything I have read on Blake and Job; perhaps Martin Buber sheds more light than anyone else in *The Prophetic Faith,* although he does not speak of Blake. The method by which Wesley and Blake handle Old Testament characters could be described first as an extension of a rather common method by which certain Old Testament characters (Joshua and Joseph, for example) are read as types of Christ. The extension of this method as they employ it is uncommon, and is of interest in assessing their place in Biblical interpretation, a place Blake claimed for himself, and I claim for Wesley. To stop with this typological idea, however, gives an inadequate and even a misleading description of the poetic result. Samuel (Wesley says or suggests) was a prophet of the Most High, trapped in time, led of God to do harm to God's people at their own insistence, instructed to anoint the wrong man before he was told to anoint the right man. When Saul came by night to a witch whose magic he himself had outlawed to practice that divination he had declared illegal, he deliberately used her powers to summon the retributive spirit of the law, the ghost of Samuel, to pronounce his fate. The Law spoke what seemed to be an unequivocal prophecy of doom. "Tomorrow shalt thou and thy sons be with me." But the Witch of Endor, in risking her life to obey her king who was near to madness, defeat, and death, performed a deed that was a manifestation of grace, an act of mercy. And the doom was prophecy of eternal life, reunited with the good Samuel and the beloved Jonathan. Wesley by-passes all legal problems of Saul's failure to make formal statement of repentance, his suicide, his rebellion against God, and makes the words of his doom into a parallel of the words of Christ, "Today thou shalt be with me in paradise."

a loved father, a brilliant and affectionate brother who had been his master at Westminster, his own child prodigy. It was the name also of a grandson he never knew, a great cathedral organist. This Samuel Wesley was born outside the law, but we remember him to the tune of "The Church's One Foundation." It is grandiose thinking to imagine oneself and one's son prophets and the sons of prophets; one is lost in the *O altitudo* of enthusiasm, the word meaning both height and depth. But neither Wesley nor Blake was a "prophet" in any sense they reserved to themselves. Blake wanted all men to be prophets, their imagination fully alive, every act truly creative. Nothing in the Wesley myth was peculiar property of Wesleys. All babies were prophets. Even those who knew not God were known of Him. Born into homes that knew not God, they might speak unwittingly for Him. In the night, God would call them by name as Samuel had been called, and Wesley taught them all to answer as Samuel had answered:

> Thine, O Lord, I surely am;
> But to me unknown Thou art;
> Come, and call me by my name,
> Whisper to my listening heart;
> Stir me up to seek Thy face,
> Claim me in my tender years,
> Manifest Thy word of grace;
> Speak, for now Thy servant hears. (vi 415)

This frame of mind, if it is mystic, if it is merely grandiose, is liable to forget that the Infant Samuels have to eat. Not Charles Wesley.

Blake speaks of a chimney sweeper as a black *thing*, and Martin Nurmi has documented that one word with shocking testimony of how accurate Blake was in his irony. These children were looked upon as inhuman.[22] In just such terms the children of the Kingswood colliers were described to John Wesley and Whitefield, and it was in response to a dare that a school was established at that place: "These untamable animals cannot hear your message, for they are brutalized and degraded below human level." Blake's picture of life among the chimney sweepers is neither realistic nor allegorical; it is real and mythic. Intricate lines of association allow the pastoral myth to pervade and control the whole carefully wrought book. It was realistic neither in literary method nor in social program for Charles Wesley to teach those ferocious and derelict lambs to sing of how they should be "To all their paradise restored," "Spotless, and peaceable, and kind." Juvenile crime

[22] Martin K. Nurmi, "Fact and Symbol in 'The Chimney Sweeper' of Blake's *Songs of Innocence*," *Bulletin of The New York Public Library* LXVIII (April 1964) 249–256.

statistics of 1788 or 1827 or 1965 prove how miserably they failed, both of
them.

One of Wesley's favorite texts was "For who hath despised the day of small
things?" Others have used it, some to remind smallness that it was being
kindly noticed, some as a reminder to do the detail work conscientiously, to
take care of the pence and so on. Wesley, as always, used it within its own
myth, evoking the narrative power of the series of events within which it
stands. The words are part of the eight visions of Zechariah (4:10) telling of
the building of Jerusalem after the Captivity. This is the myth Blake used in
what has been called a perfect Methodist hymn, the opening quatrains of
Milton.[23] "Nor shall my sword sleep in my hand / Till we have built Jerusalem." For Jerusalem after its fall must be built again by men who stand
with sword in hand. The shepherd King first built the City in more peaceful
days, but the New Jerusalem must be built for the Lamb by men who fight
even as they build. Wesley, more urgently than Blake, called the small things
to stand with Nehemiah in the company of heroes, to prophesy and see
visions with Zechariah, to build with Zerubbabel. Wesley thought they had
to do it for themselves, and do it in company, and as long as he lived he kept
the rambunctious young enthusiasts within the Establishment. Blake did not
agree. But if any little reestablished enthusiasts ever get around to doing
that job of building, they may find on the battlements a snub-nosed ghost
still restless in mental fight.

Yes, it is true that their answers differ. But with an urgency that no other
poet felt, they raised the same question: "Now, what about these children?"
Their concern may lie outside the bounds of artistic criticism, may be a
quality of the men rather than the poets. And so may their busyness in
inextinguishable hope and energy. The poetic method is the same. Such
answers as will be found will come as men perceive by the imagination those
stories that are running concurrent with life. The poets ask that the events
of life be seen as part of a coherent series of events taking place not in the
past but in eternity and containing all who exist in time.

[23] William Gaunt, *Arrows of Desire* (London 1956) 52; J. Ernest Rattenbury, *Wesley's Legacy
to the World* (London 1927) 251. Dr Rattenbury is the authority on the theology of Charles
Wesley's hymns, sensitive to every theological implication, and one I am happy to cite on
Blake's enthusiasm.

2 *HYMNS FOR THE NATION* AND *MILTON*

But then I rais'd up Whitefield, Palamabron raisd up Westley,
And these are the cries of the Churches before the two Witnesses'
Faith in God the dear Saviour who took on the likeness of men:
Becoming obedient to death, even the death of the Cross
The Witnesses lie dead in the Street of the Great City
No Faith is in all the Earth: the Book of God is trodden under Foot:
He sent his two Servants Whitefield & Westley; were they Prophets
Or were they Idiots or Madmen? shew us Miracles!

Can you have greater Miracles than these? Men who devote
Their lifes whole comfort to intire scorn & injury & death
Awake thou sleeper on the Rock of Eternity   Albion awake (117, 729)

THERE was a time not long ago when I kept saying to David Erdman that there were relations between Blake and the hymns of Wesley, and whenever he asked where they might be seen, I suggested that he look at *Hymns for the Nation.* Dr Erdman was not (visibly) impressed by my enthusiasm. Then he went to visit Sir Geoffrey Keynes, who showed him Blake's own copy of *Hymns for the Nation,* autographed "W Blake 1790." A book is a solid fact, and this essay is based on at least one solid fact, the existence of that very interesting relic.[1]

Perversity, not prescience, made me name that particular book. It was not widely popular, and I had no idea that Blake had ever seen it. Passages from Blake contradict every opinion expressed by Wesley on the American Revolution, the subject of the hymns. It is Wesley's worst book, and I say so not wholly on the grounds of his consigning my forebears to hell. But it is short, and it is full of those faults which are characteristic of Blake. Faults are more obvious than virtues, and I chose to base my argument on the obvious: the special temptations that beset a poet who is an enthusiast.

---

[1] Blake's copy is the first of two issues of *Hymns for the Nation, In 1782.* The seventeen hymns appear with minor changes in Osborn, VIII 281–308. The second issue had fourteen additional hymns (VIII 309–336). I am grateful to Sir Geoffrey Keynes for making it possible for me to compare the texts.

I have avoided problems of joint authorship in the hymns; my quotations are from Charles Wesley. I make, however, no doctrinal distinction whatsoever between the two brothers. I regard Wesley doctrine as completely unified.

[63]

Blake's autograph in *Hymns for the Nation* proves that he knew from 1790 on that he was in no obvious way *united* with the Wesleys by those traits which have been ascribed jointly to him and John Wesley: "desire for political revolution," "anarchy," "hatred of organized religion," "antinomianism," "excessive individualism." With whatever justice the traits may be assigned to Blake, they were in no obvious way Wesley traits. *Hymns for the Nation* declares the unswerving loyalty to King, Constitution, and Church of two men who lived and died High Church and High Tory.

Wesley wrote *Hymns for the Nation* when defeat for the British forces seemed almost inevitable after the collapse of Cornwallis' campaign and reverses in the West Indies at the hands of the French. The most hopeful thing he could say about the insurrection was that it was probably an instrument to punish England's rebellion against God. He saw America as Sodom, her leaders as murderers and fanatics, the Continental Congress as like Lucifer in its rage for power and its blind fury of insurrection, and he prayed for its swift removal to Tophet. The Loyalists were martyrs, persecuted by usurpers and betrayed by weak leadership of the British forces. There was a third group of Americans, those who had been intimidated by fanatics and deluded by the machinations of the world politics of Roman Catholicism. He prayed they might be given grace to return to their true allegiance even in defeat, that King George might be sent a general who would yet lead his armies to victory, that he might see his children submit themselves in "duteous piety" to their parents, his subjects show themselves obedient, his colonies brought into subjection. He prayed, but not very hopefully, "For the Conversion of the French," suggesting in his petition that it might be a good idea for God to extirpate that lustful and insolent nation from the map of Europe, and replace it with a new nation made up of the Ten Lost Tribes, "just" Jews, and converted American Indians, which group would be by nature strongly pro-British and would make an ally for a repentent Britain. "Then shall Thy whole design be seen" in an apocalyptic vision of England's place in world history.[2]

Blake called the revolutionary spirit in America Orc, the lover who can rouse the Dark Virgin who is the Muse of History and make fruitful man's

---

[2] Yet instruments of Thy design,
  The Kingdom is not theirs, but Thine,
  Who dost, with wisdom deep, employ
  The foes each other to destroy,
  And use, beyond their own intent,
  To shock, and purge the Continent.
Extirpating th'ungodly race,
  With whom wilt Thou supply their place?
  With Israel's tribes so long conceal'd?
  Just Jews, and real Christians fill'd?
  With savages, through Jesus' blood
  Redeem'd, and seal'd the sons of God? (VIII 307)

Compare Blake's marginalia on Watson's *Apology* (604). "To Extirpate a nation by means of another nation is as wicked as to destroy an individual by means of another individual which sense of time. The only just wars were waged by this generating and creating impulse in opposition to such a father-priest-king figure as Wesley pictures. Blake saw the American leaders under Washington not as Albion's enemies, but as allies of that visionary spirit of liberated energy as it existed in Britain. He thought the French intervention in America was prompted not by Roman Catholic politics but by an impulse toward freedom akin to this same spirit in Britain and America. Wesley and Blake make use of parallels between contemporary racial groups and Biblical peoples, and it would be possible to establish a relation between the poets on this basis. Possible, but fallacious.[3]

God considers (in the Bible) as Murder & commands that it shall not be done." Watson in his text had used the word *exterminate*. Blake may have recalled Wesley's word *extirpate*. Like Wesley, he cites the authority of God and cites the Bible as God's word from which all things must be proved. Unlike Wesley, Blake read as ironic *all* parts of the Bible where vengeance appears to be sanctioned; where something called *God* by men was said to have commanded genocide, Blake read the stories as having been preserved by the Holy Spirit to demonstrate man's evil, and man's projection of his own evil upon a god which was not the true God. He gave this reading to both Old and New Testaments.

[3] The mere presence of the Anglo-Israelite theory in poetry has been used to prove various characteristics of Wesley and Blake by critics who have, I fear, narrowed their minds by reading only good literature, an error Blake did not commit. In comic strips and anthropology, people are always finding the Ten Lost Tribes. Curiosity about this racial mystery indicates no specific degree of scientific acumen or religious orthodoxy, nor is it reserved to any historical era since the Diaspora. Before America was discovered, Europeans imagined a land lay to the west inhabited by Canaanites. See Howard Mumford Jones, *O Strange New World* (New York 1964) p 4. When later the American Indians were seen and described, the still unsolved mystery of their racial origin encouraged association with that other racial mystery. The idea was given freakish emphasis by Richard Brothers, but Blake had no need to find his source there; reputable anthropologists believed the descendents of the Tribes survived in England or North America, were the Highland clans (Gaunt, p 35) or the American Indians. This morning's *Times* (July 28 1965) carries a long account of a pageant being given by the Mormons in Palmyra, New York, named for the city once thought to have been built by Solomon (a theory now thought untenable, but inspiring to many poets). Nightly in up-state New York the fall of the ancient city of Zarahemia is accomplished with Blakean stage effects in stereophonic sound and modern lighting techniques. "And did those feet, etc. . . . ?" Yes. The luminous figure of Christ, as He taught in North America, appears in the pageant. Two million Mormons believe that this story was recorded by the angel Meroni, who survived the disaster, on gold tablets, the tablets having been found by Joseph Smith. Serious belief in this version of Israel's fate is not widespread outside the Mormon congregations; but that does not prove that Ezra Taft Benson, George Romney, and Stewart Udall are incompetent or do not believe in the creative power of God.

As for its use in poetry, *Hiawatha* is not uninfluenced by the idea. Parallels between England and Biblical races in poetic or allegorical form are almost as old as English poetry. In the eighteenth century, much of this writing was modeled on Watts's *Imitations of the Psalms of David*, the establishing of the parallels being one of the aims of that book. The parallels are stated there in Calvinist terms, by Christopher Smart in his psalms modeled on Watts's in orthodox terms but less Calvinist vocabulary, and restated in *Jubilate Agno* where the theory is joined with Smart's esoteric reading. Smart was not sane when he wrote *Jubilate Agno* but he believed in the creative power of God. To prove Blake mad, his work an omnium gatherum of floating absurdities, his status as a heresiarch, the offensiveness of his nationalistic arrogance all may be possible; but his use of this theory (and figures of speech from hermetic writing, the idea of incarnation, the hope that one's native land may be God's country) he had in common with men who have been considered sensible, inoffensive, and orthodox.

What *Hymns for the Nation* has in common with Blake is belligerence, exuberance, excess. These traits were not always kept under the control of poetic technique. Blake made varied uses of the Anglo-Israelite theory, and some are effective. Beautiful lyric passages sing of how "every English child" is Jerusalem-born (170). Cacaphonous listings of the "tribes" are effective in a different way; they are Blake's poetic cursing of all that separates man from man (140, 150, 151, etc). The ugly names he chooses form a contrast (and were meant to) with Milton's euphonious namings. As time (history) and space (geography) are fallen and accursed, Blake's very sounds prove that all which divides man from man causes the poet's tongue to stumble. The dimension of height and depth and breadth must be redeemed. All "numberings of the tribes" are another form of numerology. When the tribes were numbered at Mt Sinai, that numbering did not serve to prove to Israel how strong she was, but rather served promptly as proof of her weakness in her own eyes. Israel could not enter the Promised Land until every man counted at Sinai had died. As in a phonic parable, Blake is asking that his own numerology be forgiven. At the close of *Jerusalem* these numberings vanish, foregone and forgiven, as he forgives Bacon and Newton and Locke for theirs. The mutual forgiveness accomplished, fountains of water rise from the flames, and the poetry itself, in sublime imagistic and tonal logic, becomes as flame and water.

But at times his Druids are bombast. His historical parallels at times are a distraction and a *gêne*. Wesley's plan for replacing the French with the Ten Lost Tribes does not appeal to me. It seems extravagant. His hymns on the Gordon Riots and the American Revolution are extravagant. Violent imagery portrays interplanetary storm and showers of fire. His cosmos is cluttered with figures such as one sees in broken-line drawings of the constellations. The air is full of sweeping besoms and chariots and whirlwinds. Enormous feet make footprints all over earth and sea and abyss. There are mass migrations and racial dislocations. The formulae of ancient magic are suggested: the magic power of naming, the efficacy of a man's death, "dominion" springing from a man-like body as a growing tree or a flowing fountain. These ideas were used elsewhere by Wesley in less hectic poetry. "Arm of the Lord, awake, awake!" as it was published in 1739 was a fine hymn based on Isaiah 51. When it was revised to comment on the Gordon Riots, decorum did not govern energy. The recurrent image of a great arm holding a sword or a scourge as it is used in *Hymns for the Nation* represents both a diminution of poetic energy and a loss of control of technique. In both poets, there were similar intellectual and emotional pressures that

explode through vulnerable places in technique; and both occasionally substitute bombast when energy flags. They were liable to be at their worst
or at their very best when they wrote of the Great Awakening.

Blake's poem *Milton* tells of the error made by that great poet in his earthly
life when he represented God as a vengeful deity. The power of Milton's
poetry had contributed to the despair that had seized upon men thereafter.
Under the driving of Satan, many men (Voltaire and Rousseau among them)
sought escape from despair by asserting the self-righteousness of man. The
spirit of Milton, perceiving the harm he had done, entered into the poet
William Blake to declare his errors and make amends by speaking through
Blake's poetry a corrected version of man's history (which story is the epic
Jerusalem) and truly justifying the ways of God to men.

Los, spirit of prophecy, summoned his two sons, Palamabron and Rintrah,
who are associated with the Two Witnesses of the Book of Revelation, and
with the two figures, Moses and Elijah, who stood with the transfigured
Christ. Palamabron (Moses), symbol of pity, is the redeemed spirit of the
law as contrasted with the deadly letter of the law, a value assigned by Blake
to Aaron and the priestly office. Rintrah (Elijah) is symbol of righteous
wrath. Palamabron, like Moses, is the type of prophet who can work within
a social order; Rintrah is the reprobate, the hermit, the rebel, the outcast
from society.

Palamabron and Rintrah "rais'd up" Wesley and Whitefield. This expression is common in the Old Testament and signifies men specially called to
meet a crisis in history. The symbolic values of Rintrah and Palamabron
are transferred to Whitefield and Wesley. Whitefield was a more rebellious
spirit, who, unlike the Wesleys, left the Anglican church. Blake's choice of
John Wesley as type of a prophet able to work within a social order is one
more example added to many examples of Blake's deep knowledge of his
own age. The story of the Two Witnesses now is made to apply to the two
evangelists.[4] According to the account in Revelation, the Gentiles shall

---

[4] Those critics who read Blake as a satirist of the Methodists may like to pursue a line of inquiry
that could perhaps result in reading this passage also as sardonic. How much did he know of
the mad and blood-stained annals of enthusiasm on the Continent? The story of "The Two
Witnesses of Berne" was a famous one, and he may be comparing Whitefield and Wesley to
those two degenerate freaks; the idea is no more far-fetched than some criticism of
Blake I have read. Two brothers in Switzerland claimed to be the Two Witnesses of
Revelation, revived gnostic teachings, set up a completely cynical trade in indulgences,
were exiled, returned secretly, were apprehended, and one was strangled and his body
publicly burned, not for his beliefs, but for horrible crimes committed by him and encouraged
in his followers. See Karl Rudolph Hagenbach, *History of the Church in the Eighteenth and
Nineteenth Centuries*, 2 vols (New York 1869) I 195 *et passim*, for other parallels. That
Wesley discipline represented to Blake a castration of the spirit is a provocative idea; there was
a chiliastic sect in Russia called the Castrators, who thought the Judgment Day could not come

"tread under foot" the holy city during a period of time when the Two Witnesses are protected by God until their testimony is completed. Then "the beast which ascendeth out of the bottomless pit" shall kill them, "And their dead bodies shall lie in the streets of the great city, which spiritually is called Sodom and Egypt, where also our Lord was crucified." After three and a half days, the Two Witnesses live again and are called up to heaven while an earthquake destroys a tenth part of the city.

Even this brief passage shows the similarity of Blake's method to the Apocalyptic method. The author of Revelation cites the Destruction of the Cities of the Plain, the Captivity in Egypt, and the Crucifixion, and uses that principle of double meanings adopted by Blake. Jerusalem is at once the holy city and the equivalent of Sodom and Egypt, for it was actually in Jerusalem that "our Lord was crucified." Blake further interweaves the story with allusions to Hosea, Jesus and the Pharisees, Moses and Pharaoh, Jonah, and Paul before Agrippa.[5] The Hebrew prophets confront some form

---

until 144,000 persons had been castrated (this is the apocalyptic numbering of the saints), and set busily about the task. To speak somewhat less sardonically, the place to begin with any real study would be a comparison of *An Island in the Moon* with Albert M. Lyles, *Methodism Mocked: The Satiric Reaction to Methodism in the Eighteenth Century* (London 1960). Blake later praised Hervey, Whitefield, Wesley, Methodists, and enthusiasm; but here, in a close approximation of Augustan satire, he has one of his eccentrics read Hervey; another reports her ecstatic reaction to an enthusiastic preacher. Locke is mentioned derisively. But it is not possible to lump all the subjects mentioned in *An Island in the Moon* as things Blake did not care for. One must look at his other writings. He did not care for Locke's ideas, and made that opinion amply clear elsewhere. From Blake's address "To the Deists," it is clear that he did not consider Whitefield a contemptible figure, though he did laugh at Mr Huffcap. It is certain that Blake knew Samuel Foote's stage satires of Whitefield; from parts of *An Island in the Moon* it might be thought that he knew Foote's other work. Compare the account of Chatterton (Chapter 5) with Foote's story of the Grand Panjandrum, which you learned in the nursery, though you may not have associated it with Foote. But Blake's attitude toward Chatterton was not derisive. He made very serious and sympathetic use of Chatterton's work. Incidentally, the "anthems" in *An Island in the Moon* are very interesting lyrics, and I should like to know what tunes he had in mind when he wrote them.

[5] See the lines quoted at the head of this essay. Rintrah speaks first. Then, confronted by the Two Witnesses' faith in God, the Churches cry: "Becoming . . . Miracles." Then Rintrah speaks again: "Can . . . awake, etc." The words "the likeness of men," are quoted from Philippians 4:7. The words, "Becoming obedient unto death, even the death of the cross," are a continuation of that quotation. They are a deliberately ambivalent modifier, referring both to "God the dear Savior," to whom both phrases apply in Philippians, and grammatically modifying *Witnesses* in the next line, making the "martyrdom" of Whitefield and Wesley a type of the Crucifixion. Blake alludes to Hosea 9:7, where the prophet speaks of Egypt as enemy of Israel. "The days of recompence are come; Israel shall know it: the prophet is a fool, the spiritual man is mad." "Shew a miracle" are Pharaoh's words to Moses (Ex 7:9). The Pharisees and Sadducees tempted Jesus, "desiring him that he would shew them a sign from heaven," and he said, "A wicked and adulterous generation seeketh after a sign; and there shall no sign be given unto it but the sign of the prophet Jonah," that is, resurrection after three days (Matt 12:36 and 16:4). When Paul before Agrippa spoke of the resurrection, Festus called him mad (Acts 26:23–25), and Paul appealed to King Agrippa's faith in the prophets. Other passages may be alluded to (Heb 2:16–17; I Corinthians 3:18, e.g.) where the foolishness of

of authority that is associated with Egypt, Babylon, or Rome, or with ecclesiastical authority. These symbols unite with the term *the Churches* to form that which Blake called the Elect, a term which will be discussed later. The request of the Elect for a sign is a reiterated situation in his poetry. The Elect "cannot believe in Eternal Life / Except by Miracles & a New Birth" (121). It was the New Birth that was the message of Whitefield and the Wesleys in the revival called the Great Awakening, and Blake in this passage is placing them in the direct line of the prophets, and is contradicting especially the deist dogma on the subject of revelation. Blake's interpretation of the evil "Mystery" is his own, but it is based on interpretations that have been standard since Jerome wrote.[6] Blake disdained historical allegory, and interpreted the Bible by "Spiritual Mystery," or "spiritually," as the author of Revelation says. He felt no less and no more responsibility to the facts of geography and history than did John on Patmos, who was incorrect in saying that the Crucifixion took place in Sodom; but all the facts in the story are important, and the place of each story in Biblical history and interpretation is always of first importance. Blake is incorrect when he says that the bodies of Whitefield and Wesley lay about London streets in this unsanitary manner; they died decently in bed and were not martyrs.[7]

---

belief in the resurrection is said to be wisdom. The "Churches" are the seven churches of Asia Minor to whom Revelation (1:4, 11) is addressed. The story of the Two Witnesses is in Revelation 11.

[6] Blake's source for this use of the word Mystery is Rev 17, the only use in the Bible where the word has sinister meaning. The context indicates that the evil city must stand in relation to Jews and Christians at the time of writing as Babylon stood in relation to the ancient Hebrew nation. Jerome interpreted the word on the forehead of the Great Whore to stand for Rome, the blasphemies being the assumption of divinity by the emperors. I Peter 5:13 is also glossed by interpreting Babylon to mean Rome. Rome, Babylon, and Egypt are powers that enslave, and remove the faithful from the true city, the true bride. The Puritan interpretation combined the two ideas of political and religious authority, but differed by making the Beast to mean ancient Rome and the Woman to represent Roman Catholicism. The passage is thus glossed in the Geneva Bible: "The beast signifieth y ancient Rome; y woman y sitteth thereo y new Rome w' is the Papistrie whose crueltie w' bloodshedding is declared by *skarlat*." Blake keeps the two root ideas of religious and civil authority, and adds his own meaning: abstract thought with its inhuman tyranny, and that blurring of vision which comes from viewing the true "Spiritual Mystery" with the eyes of abstract thought. In Blake's poetry, the "priests" seem to represent the false Mystery, and the monks the "Spiritual Mystery." See *Jerusalem* 52 and "The Gray Monk." By his principle of contraries, he gave the word Mystery both high and low meanings. In *The Vision of the Last Judgment* (545) "Spiritual Mystery" is source of the highest art.

[7] The Wesleys were the properest martyrs for their age. Trained in an Age of Classicism, they even went back to the Greek root, *witnesses*. In an Age of Common Sense, they were neither teetotalers nor addicts about suffering and dying for the cause; they could take it or leave it. They were fearless, but unaware of heroism as a man is unaware of a healthy skin. In an Age of Reason, they pursued their logic to the grave; they had meant what they said. In an Age of Gentlemen, they did not take on, but just died, polite as can be to all present, rejoicing in

Wesley's association with scholarly analysis of the Bible began in early childhood; Blake's knowledge of the Bible was a fruit of independent study. Their verbal memories were what we call "gifts," and each in his own way disciplined that gift until the result seems not so much the power of total recall as physical digestion. John on Patmos was commanded to eat the Book as a preliminary to his writing of the Apocalypse. Wesley and Blake write as if the Book has been assimilated into nerve and sinew. They use it with complete consistency always, yet with great freedom, testing it by satire, proving it by the contraries of thought and life, finding it applicable to the great issues and to the minutiae of life, fitting its words into their own meters as if the Word belonged there. Wesley is famous for his intricate patterns of cross-reference. There are short lyrics that shine with surface candor and simplicity and contain as many as fifty allusions to passages culled from Genesis to Revelation, each used with full responsibility for their doctrinal interpretation and for the plot-lines of the stories alluded to.[8] Blake's patterns of cross-reference are comparable in method but less intricate.

They thought the universal truth of the Bible could absorb other truth. Wesley did not absorb such vast amounts of extra-Biblical material as Blake used, and he aspired to be known as *homo unius liberi*, but the tracing of his allusions shows that he did not deserve that title in any restrictive sense.[9] The Bible story as used by both men carried intricate thought and doctrine, Wesley's being the more intricate, for all its surface simplicity.[10]

---

the Lamb. So did Blake, witnessing to his faith in the divinity of man and the eternal nature of art, saying, "I will draw your portrait, Kate." Truth, orthodox or unorthodox, sits upon the lips of dying men. Blake could have said nothing more absolutely consistent with all he had ever said. John Wesley said, "And the best of all is God with us." Charles, too weak to write, dictated a silly little hymn about a joke he liked, a gnostic notion that Blake liked too, the idea that heaven is beneath man. He had written better hymns about it, but they always sound rather childish, and always imply a story, a myth, about how he would fall, like a child falling from the branches of a Tree, catching at a branch for a moment, then falling again, until clunk! he hit those Arms. Now at last, they all thought, they would see quite clearly the face of love loved so long; Blake could draw God at any time. Drawing God was a simple matter compared to drawing Kate.

[8] "With glorious clouds incompast round" (VII 26) has fifty allusions. See W. F. Moultrie, *Proceedings of the Wesley Historical Society* I (1897) 26–27.

[9] Champion explicator of allusions is Henry Bett, *The Hymns of Methodism* 3rd ed (London 1945).

[10] I am aware of statements about Wesley "simplicity." Ronald Knox, *Enthusiasm* (Oxford 1950) 515, says the Wesley message was simple because it "left nine-tenths of Christian doctrine out of consideration, and concentrated on the remaining tenth — soteriology." It is questionable whether or not soteriology is a mere tithe of the doctrine. Father Knox speaks of John Wesley's sermons; he seems never to have heard of the hymns. The Wesleys preached as presbyters of the Church of England, bringing their converts to the Establishment. They did not

Their poetry is prophetic and evangelical, the messages are intensely personal and aimed at reformation of the social order. They meant to bring about an inner change, in the heart, in the imagination, and hoped that social changes would come about as a result. They call to a Great Awakening. Blake's challenge in *Milton* is "England, awake! awake! awake!" and his refrain is, "Mark well my words! they are of your eternal salvation." They did not want the Lamp unto man's feet to be dimmed by the Enlightenment.

The middle ground from which the poets are clearly different can be charted by some consideration of the authorities they acknowledged. The differences are obvious and important, but some of them have been exaggerated. An obvious difference is Wesley's acknowledged obligation to clarity. He wrote in three traditions that demanded it. The Augustan esthetic demanded it, and he added to that demand his own emphasis on the didactic nature of his writings and the nature of the audience he addressed, for his hymns were frankly a means of teaching so large a thing as Christian doctrine and so small a thing as vocabulary. Where he used an unusual word, he meticulously defined it in the next line. The hymn tradition itself demanded clarity because of its dedication to general congregational use. And the insistence of Protestants upon clear understanding of all religious services was the chief reason for the shift to the vernacular. None of these pressures operated directly upon Blake. He would not accede to demands for a certain sort of "clarity," for it involved the writer in those generalizations which seemed to him a blurring of true clarity.

The authority exercised over a work of art by its audience is a point of difference. Wesley's awareness of and acknowledgement of this authority was much greater than Blake's. They have been made examples of both extremes in this matter; Wesley's style has been accounted for by his philistine commitment to the utility of art, and the change of Blake's style has been

---

preach as founders of a church, but stressed what seemed to them a classic doctrine of the Church that was being neglected in the Church. The sermons do not elaborate on doctrines not then in question. It has been demonstrated by Catholics and Protestants, however, that the sermons do carry the full doctrine. See for example M. Piette, *John Wesley and the Evolution of Protestantism*, and John M. Todd, *John Wesley and the Catholic Church*. It is true that the sermons do not give extended treatment to such subjects as the Trinity, Christology, the deity of the Holy Spirit, and it is true that these doctrines when they are treated are placed in relation to soteriology, as is proper according to the doctrine. The hymns differ from the sermons in that they make much fuller statement of these doctrines because they would not be dealt with in church song of that day. There are, for example, two volumes of *Hymns on the Trinity*. The richness of doctrinal statement in the hymns has been studied many times, J. E. Rattenbury's work being a case in point. The general conclusion is that any alteration whatsoever impoverishes the logic and the fullness of the doctrine. In its full statement, it is not a simple doctrine.

accounted for by his failure to command an audience.[11] I think both extremes have been exaggerated, and I think that any final statement on the subject would necessarily involve one in vain and fruitless surmise about how they might have written had their circumstances been other than they were. But the difference is marked. As things are, it is not difficult to see that Wesley's poetry is something Blake's is not — part of an hour-by-hour dialogue between artist and audience, a social instrument that would have been rendered useless by lack of clarity, written almost literally on the run, and written so that he who runs may read.

The authority of academic standards of excellence had no part in Blake's esthetic. He thanked God he was never sent to school. Wesley's lifelong association with scholarship was given special poignancy when it came about that his university was in his eyes one of the sources of the authorization of his ministry.[12]

Blake professed antagonism to empirical philosophy, experimental science, and the lower and higher criticism of the Bible that were an important product of the Enlightenment. Wesley accepted the ideas early in life and absorbed them into his hymns. But, rebellious or no, both were children of the Enlightenment, and their relation to these ideas was a complicated one. Blake reacted in many different ways to empiricism. His work needed a useful knowledge of physics, chemistry, measurement, anatomy. He gave eager response to the Biblical criticism in his own way. The lower and higher criticism

---

11 Other explanations of his change of style include his "growing gnosticism," his increasing assumption of a "mask of gnosticism," his "perverseness," his decision not to mirror nature because truth is not to be found in nature, his loss of the power of self-criticism, a loss of control over his poetic medium. I account for his change in style by his change of the literary genres he wrote in, and his interpretation of the nature of genres. His last poem, *The Everlasting Gospel*, which reverts to a type of satire similar to that of *An Island in the Moon*, is much clearer than *An Island*, displaying no lack of clarity and control of tone and medium, although the ideas it presents are much more complex than those in the earlier work. *Jerusalem* is indeed a much more difficult poem than the early songs, and all the prophetic books are difficult (as Daniel and Jeremiah are difficult books). But I do not observe that my students find *Milton* any more difficult or any less "self-contained" a poem than *The Dunciad*. *Jerusalem* is difficult because it assumes the reader knows London as Pope assumes it, and assumes that the reader knows the history of the Hebrews and the situation in Jerusalem as Jeremiah assumed that knowledge.

12 One of Wesley's earliest memories must have been his father's engagement in comparing all versions of Job in all available Oriental languages. He had the tutelage of his older brother Samuel at home and at Westminster School. His hymns demonstrate his thorough training in translation, prosody, formal logic, the intricate classification of figures of speech; these studies were the center of the curriculum. John Wesley, when his right to preach was challenged, claimed a *jus ubique praecandi* as a member of the university. I am not sure that this law (even as John Wesley made the claim) covered Charles Wesley, who was not a Fellow, as John Wesley was. And I am not sure that such a law existed even for Fellows. There was a *jus ubique docendi* allowing Fellows to teach anywhere. Still, it is true that they took some authentication of their ministry as being from that source, and took the world as parish.

had a wide basis in linguistic studies, and he learned Hebrew and Greek in order to study the Bible in response to that emphasis. It was based on Oriental studies and explorations and excavations that brought to public attention much esoteric and exotic information which he made use of. Work in the higher criticism on the Continent and in England was concentrated upon the literary genres of the Bible. This type of inquiry was widely known to the public from the early eighteenth century.[13] Wesley's father was involved in it. Watts and Wesley, trained rhetoricians, nourished their infant genre of the English hymn with such strength as could be poured into it from pastoral, ode, neoclassical imitation, epic, satire, and from the prose genres of the sermon and the tract. Blake responded in one manner by finding in the Bible the whole span of literary forms. In the Book were his models for all descriptions of all sins, crude humor, subtle irony, petulant complaint, grandiose praise, exalted lyricism, pain like vivisection, worldly opinion and unworldly wisdom, earthy and unearthly passion.

Wesley looked upon himself as transmitting a received dogma. Blake claimed no connection with any existing orthodoxy, but he was a more extreme example of bibliolatry than Wesley. The general Protestant devotion to its "paper pope" has always been visibly intensified in Britain, and Wesley and Blake are good examples of that devotion. But Wesley (and Milton) took into their poetry an inspiration from classical models and a literary reverence for "the gods of Priam"; they did not derogate classical art in order to praise the Bible.[14] Blake's doctrine came by direct revelation, but

[13] Since the pastoral is the genre discussed at greatest length in this essay, I illustrate by the theory of Charles Claud Genest (1639–1731), a French theologian, who said that Theocritus modeled his pastorals on the Song of Solomon. English scholars adopted the theory, among them the father of the Wesleys. Anthony Blackwall put the theory in his *Introduction to the Classics*, the most highly respected textbook of rhetoric in this period, and from 1718 on, the theory was common in the classrooms. Milton in *The Reason of Church Government* gives Job as example of the epic, the Song of Solomon (citing Origen as authority) as pastoral, and the Apocalypse as example of tragedy, a statement that is repeated in the introduction of *Samson Agonistes*. But genre study took a much more secular form, even when these studies were pursued by the devout. Those who studied the pastoral as a literary genre of the Bible include Bossuet and Genest in France; in England, Bishop Percy, Bishop Lowth, and Thomas Harmer; in Germany, J. D. Michaelis and Herder.

[14] *Milton* opens: "The Stolen and Perverted Writings of Homer & Ovid: of Plato & Cicero. which all Men ought to contemn: are set up by artifice against the Sublime of the Bible" (94). From *A Vision of the Last Judgment* (545): "the Greek Fables originated in Spiritual Mystery the Greek Gospel are Genuine Preserved by the Saviours Mercy." Blake went beyond the position of Thomas Taylor, as is shown by George Harper Mills, *The Neoplatonism of William Blake* & Real Visions Which are lost & clouded in Fable & Alegory <while> the Hebrew Bible & (Chapel Hill 1961) 195–197. He also went beyond the statements of Milton, Watts, or the Blake told H. C. Robinson that all he knew was in the Bible, a statement, one takes it, to be read "spiritually," rather than for its historical or geographical accuracy. See *Blake, Coleridge, Wordsworth, Lamb, etc., being Selections from the Remains of Henry Crabb Robinson*, ed Wesleys in his insistence that classic art was a degenerate copy of the work of Asian patriarchs.

the doctrine had to do with exegesis of the Bible. He cited the Bible as final proof of all he alleged. He placed the Hebrew and the Greek Testaments together at the very height of art and sanctity. He did not claim to be a mystic, and did not use the word.[15] He claimed to be a visionary, an enthusiast, and a Christian, and defined the terms carefully. I have read, and now am reading in newspapers, statements of literary critics and those who call themselves "atheistic theologians" to the effect that Blake had no god but man. People who are not atheists are usually willing to leave to God such important judgments about others. On this subject, as on other statements about himself, Blake seems clear enough. He said always and passionately that he was a Christian, and I know only One who has a better right to an opinion on that subject.

He was an enthusiast. The usual way of categorizing enthusiasts is according to their acceptance or rejection of previous revelation.[16] Some, like the Babis, do not value previous revelation. Some, like the Muslims or the Mormons, in supplementing previous revelation, tend to supercede it. Some attach themselves to previous revelation; of this type, the Hebrew prophets are the noblest examples, and Blake claimed to belong to this type.

Edith J. Morley (Manchester 1922) 12. Blake's statements form part of contemporary controversy. No brief summary of the positions of Bacon, Newton, and Locke with reference to the Bible is satisfactory (Watts on Locke is very interesting), but some specific points of controversy may be stated. Bacon, *The Advancement of Learning* (Oxford 1920) 102–103, says that the parables of Jesus were intended to obscure spiritual truths to the eyes of all but a chosen few; Blake thought the parables were revelations of truth to all men, operating through the power of the stories to bring into play man's imagination. Newton and Locke, both in private studies and in their letters to one another, concentrate their attention on the Apocalypse, and Newton thought his efforts to establish the chronology of the Bible and the Greek myths were probably his most important work. Blake distrusted such thinking. Mathematical speculation "cages" the imagination in unspiritual "Mystery" of abstract thought. Sects that indulge in it (and there were many in Blake's time) and in numerology, and predictions of the Second Coming, illustrate by their histories that such "law" may be, as Blake said, based on an essential lawlessness. Blake associated eighteenth-century rationality with this form of mystification. Even title pages of Blake's day illustrate his meaning. *An Attempt to Translate the Prophetic Parts of the Apocalypse of Saint John into Familiar Language by Divesting it of the Metaphors in Which It Is Involved* (Boston 1794) by James Winthrop, son of "the Late professor of mathematics," is an illustration. Divesting himself of metaphors, the author soon converts from poetic figures to mathematical digits. This is the type of mystification in the name of clarity to which Blake addressed his arguments, for he regarded it as the special problem of his own day, as well as a recurrent situation in human history. Blake was not a systematic student of language theory or theology — or rather, he followed his own system in his reading; but it will not do to condescend to him where the subject is language and the use of language in his own day, the assessing of society in terms of its sense of metaphor.

[15] The Blake concordance shows two uses of the word *mystic*, both in contexts that are not significant.

[16] *Encyclopedia of Religion and Ethics,* ed James Hastings, 12 vols (New York 1912) v 317.

Masonic orders of the eighteenth century, for example, intended their dogma of the brotherhod of man to supercede the New Testament as, in their opinion, the New Testament had superceded the Old.[17] Blake held the whole canon as total truth and totally true. He intended to supercede nothing but erroneous readings of the Bible, Milton's among them, and had nothing to add to the Bible except the correct reading of what was already there. That reading was not orthodox, but it was consistent, and he held himself responsible to his own interpretation. His acceptance of the entire canon sets him apart from Ann Lea, the Muggletonians, the Swedenborgians, the deists, the Christian Scientists. His refusal to add to the truth of the scripture as he read it sets him apart from the Masons, the Mormons, the Muslims. His refusal to read the Bible as historical allegory sets him apart from Locke and Newton and the sects that subscribe to numerology.

The Bible was to Wesley and Blake the myth, the narrative, which runs concurrent with present events, explaining present events and the Last Things, and being in turn explained by the present, so that only the Word made human life comprehensible, and only the individual's life fully revealed the meaning of the Word. Neither of them used allegory. Neither recounted at length the stories from the Bible, as Milton did in his three last poems. The Bible is present by allusion, but primarily it is action that is alluded to, rather than symbol, doctrine, image. The burden of proof is on me to show that this method is in any way idiosyncratic. I have quoted enough of the book of Revelation to show how elder myths interpreted present events and the Last Things in that book. The process goes on throughout the Bible. The New Testament canticles and the song of the apostles in Acts 4:23 rephrase older writings for present purposes. When the canon of the scripture was established, the presence of such allusions was accepted as contributing evidence of canonicity. The method of thought was standard in patristic interpretations and those of the Middle Ages, and in some ways it is standard today, however casually or systematically the four levels of scripture interpretation may be employed by the writer of sermon, novel, drama, exegesis, poetry, or the script of a motion picture spectacular.

Neoclassical poetry framed current events in some myth; the relation between past and present was often ironic, the present being diminished by reference to the past (as was the purpose of *The Rape of the Lock*) or (as in *Absalom and Achitophel*) set in jesting relation. By reference to the myth, present events could be tempered into common sense and placed in reason-

---

[17] J. Bronowski's discussion of Blake's ambivalent images taken from Masonic ritual is of interest in this connection. See p 95–96.

able proportions. From this ironic usage, the myths suffered some damage, Hector by being made parallel to Belinda, King David by being made parallel to Charles II. In the poetry of Wesley and Blake, this sort of irony has no place. Current events are never diminished in importance by reference to the sublime myth (this is a distinctive characteristic of Wesley's hymns) because the present was not to be viewed by the eyes of mere "reason" or "common sense." The present was of tremendous importance: this moment is of eternal significance. Nor is the myth ever diminished. Such meaning as each saw in the Bible was held in reverent and passionate belief, and the myth infuses the present, rather than framing it.

Watts, Herbert, Milton, T. S. Eliot all were careful of doctrine, conscious of image and symbol, and none wrote in ignorance of the stories to which they allude. The doctrines differed (Wesley's and Blake's differ) but the distinction I want to make is in poetic method. In a given poem, the demand for recognizing the relation of that poem to the Bible (and all their writings are based on the Bible) may be met in different ways. Watts rested the weight of his hymns and psalms on doctrinal interpretation, as contrasted with the literal rendering that had been the ideal of earlier church music. His method gave to his best work a grandeur of generalization that is unsurpassed in hymnody. He deliberately removed the Psalmist from his particular locale and situation, thereby moving his poetry in the direction of universal doctrine. Wesley does not remove Wrestling Jacob from Jacob's situation; he immerses the reader in the patriarch's action, and it is an experience that is made universal.

Blake thought Aaron's gems had been acquired by forced tribute. Herbert and Wesley associated those gems with their daily lives, dressed themselves in them, humbly claiming their part in an eternal priesthood, not reserving virtue to the priesthood, not reserving any goodness to themselves in arrogancy. Blake's method is like Wesley's and unlike Herbert's in the demand he makes for the whole story of Aaron to be present in the reader's mind. Herbert placed great reliance on the image-making power of the mind, and the relation of his poems to the Bible can more nearly be met by imaging a collar, a pulley, a table prepared for a guest, Aaron's gems as they adorn the priestly office.

T. S. Eliot's beliefs were in general those of Herbert and Wesley, High Church and Arminian. The explication of his poetry requires much explaining of myths, but he is a symbolist, not a mythic poet. A symbolist trusts the conception of some object which need not be clearly visualized and which, even removed from its usual religious associations (as Herbert does not remove his images) has power to form a link with religious truth. For the purposes of his poetry, Eliot accepts no myth whatsoever in its totality. His poetic method is akin to the method of anthropology, upon which science he draws heavily. He analyzes all myths, choosing elements from any he needs, accepting only the part that suits his purpose. The disjunction of his "objects" from their usual associations is quite deliberate and essential for his purpose. If the reader attempts to understand his poetry in narrative terms, he is brought up short by Eliot's refusal to "mean" any story, even that of Becket. Eliot means his symbols, but not his stories. A blood brother of the neoclassical writers, he, in his way, dramatizes for us the modern loss of our faith in any myth. We must dismember, analyze, criticize, all myths in search of truth, which will come finally through a symbol, not through a story. He urges no one to act; he really thinks acting and suffering are the same thing. His poetry, like Blake's, has difficulties for the reader, but the difficulties are different and their solution is different. Blake means every story he tells, even when he maddeningly refuses to tell it. To understand Blake, one must move with his stories, both those he tells and those he implies.

The distinction between Blake and Milton was made earlier in this section by saying that Blake thought Milton erred in representing God as a vengeful deity. To go any further with the matter demands some definition of Blake's "diabolic" reading of the Bible and of his term *the Elect*. One cannot define the term by negatives, but must proceed, as Blake proceeded, by contraries. The most important idea is that Blake, while assigning to that term everything he thought was evil, by a contrary point of view, thought of himself as the Elect, "chosen," in that he was English, a prophet, and an artist. He did not choose these things; he was chosen. The contrary idea must be stressed in the same breath; first, he was what he was by his own hourly, free, and difficult choice, and he knew it. And he called in stentorian tones upon all men to chose to be what he was, and his evangelical message insists that men are free to choose.

The Elect, the Chosen, were the Jews. By covenant between God and Abraham, they became forever a nation of priests and prophets to fulfil God's purpose for man in a peculiar way so that through them all nations of the earth should be blessed. Blake thought that this race, either historically or by the reading of "Spiritual Mystery," had their origin in England and that God's purpose would manifest itself in some peculiar way there — again, his interpretation is at times historical and geographical, and at times spiritual, merely an insistence upon the importance of the here and the now: I say unto you, verily, verily, it is at Felpham, it is in London, it is in Oxford Street, that this great thing will and must take place.

There was a period of time when the great "Election" was the Catholic Church. There was a time when the Protestant "Election," especially associated with Calvin, was the power to be dreaded. In Blake's day, there was greater danger in a deist, a rationalist Elect. The most obvious and dramatic examples are to be found where civil and religious power are joined, and Blake used these examples from history. When Jewish religion had power to take vengeance, when the Catholic church had power to enforce its self-righteousness, when the Calvinists had power to revenge their wrongs, when rationalism had the reins of civil and religious power — these historical situations are dramatic and he found them usable. But what he opposes is not any institution in its entirety; and what he placed his hope in was not any institution. The "Elect" is a state, a point in a series of happenings, and it takes men and governments in its course — Blake himself not excepted. The epic struggle in *Jerusalem* is against Blake's own self-righteousness. He gives a poor report on the Law, but no worse account than lawyers have given. He gives a poor account of the Church — any church; it is confirmed by those who best love the Church. None know better than churchmen how quickly the vital experience may become a degenerate reliance upon ritualistic theurgy. There is a progress of despair ending in that ossification which places its trust only in sacred rites.

All these concessions do not place Blake within the bounds of orthodoxy. I am for the moment emphasizing his common ground with Wesley. Wesley, a good churchman, knew more. He knew the human value of sacred rites, and the human value of a human law, imperfect though both were.

Blake did not confine his denunciations to church and state. Doing away with church and state would not remove from man's nature the dreary fact. Denied expression in religious and political life, the self-righteousness of Election manifested itself in secular and private life and in art. Voltaire and Rousseau had fostered it as surely as had church and state. Reynolds represented it. Milton's errors were written down at a time in Milton's life when he had no religious affiliation and no political power. The better the artist, the more dangerous was his Election — hence Blake's choice of Milton and Reynolds. Those wars he describes, and with which he identified himself, the political uprisings in which he hoped at times, all must be fought against the father-priest-king who represented the Elect; and they must be fought for his sake. The aim of the war is the salvation of the Elect. If this is not accomplished, the war is lost, and its only result is to set up a new Elect, which will say, as the Elect always say, "I am right, and you are therefore wrong," and will exact vengeance, and will set up the deadly round of crime and punishment. This perverts the creative principle of self-sacrifice into the immolation of man's true nature by denial and asceticism (when he cannot inflict his cruelty on others, and has only himself to punish) or the ritualistic sacrifices of others to its own self-righteousness. Men deify this self-righteousness in both of its forms, and call it God. Blake calls it sometimes Jehovah, sometimes Satan (though both these names have their "good" contraries). But by any name, it is never the true God.

Asking pardon for omitting proper emphasis upon the traits that divide Wesley and Blake, I recount some well-known facts about the hymns of Charles Wesley. It has been said, and truly said, that every hymn he ever wrote was a protest against this Election. I have dutifully recorded the gravest example to the contrary, *Hymns for the Nation*; have based my essay on the proof in the Keynes library that Blake knew it. I base my arguments largely on Charles Wesley's grave faults as a poet, and quote all his worst verse. And I now compound my sins against the Wesleys by telling of their quarrels. They quarreled with Whitefield about Election and Reprobation, and made up the quarrel by saying what the Elect can never say, "That which unites us is far more important than what divides us," and Whitefield agreed, proving that he was no more a true member of the Elect than the Wesleys. But in the course of that quarrel, Charles Wesley produced some satire on the subject more pointed than any Blake ever wrote, and a more thorough description of real diabolic reading of the Bible than Blake was able to give.[18] His work had the effect of permanently mollifying

---

[18] "The Horrible Decree" (III 34–38) is satire, more than hymn. *Hymns on God's Everlasting Love*, two series, published in 1741 and 1742, match the words from Calvin's *Institutes* against the stories from the Bible that, in Wesley's opinion, refuted that doctrine. See especially the *Institutes*, Book III, Chapter 24, Sections 8 and 24; and Chapter 33, Section 7, on infant damnation: "Decretum quidem horribile fateor." These are the closing stanzas of one of Wesley's hymns. Compare with Blake's method of diabolic reading.

'Tis we, the wretched abjects, we,
  Our sin and death on Thee translate;
We think that Fury is in Thee,
  Horribly think that God is hate.

'Thou hast compell'd the lost to die;
  'Hast reprobated from Thy face;
'Hast others sav'd but them past by;
  'Or mock'd with only damning grace.'

How long, thou jealous God, how long
  Shall impious worms Thy word disprove?

Thy justice stain, thy Mercy wrong,
  Deny Thy faithfulness and love?

Still shall the HELLISH DOCTRINE stand?
  And Thee for its dire author claim?
No — let it sink at Thy command
  Down to the pit from whence it came.

Arise, O God, maintain Thy cause!
  The fulness of the Gentiles call:
Lift up the Standard of Thy Cross,
  And all shall know Thou died'st for all.

the worst form of a degenerate Calvinism. Like Blake, his chief battle was with the Elect who snatched the Bible and preëmpted it for their evil proof. And this is the whole point to Blake's "diabolic" reading of the Bible.

Calvin had grieved to record what he himself called God's Horrible Decree. Where the Decree of Election is preached with no cognizance taken of Calvin's pity, the doctrine degenerates. Watts, like Blake, refused to admit that the idea of vengeance was appropriate for Christians, and he omitted many Psalms and parts of Psalms that used the theme.[19] Blake was more orthodox than Watts; he omitted nothing. Watts made no secret of how he searched the Bible for refutation of the belief in eternal punishment, could not find it, sadly reported what he found, and said as little about it as conscience would allow. One of John Wesley's most effective publications in the quarrel with Whitefield was a pamphlet of quotations from the Calvinist Watts. In the definitive Wesley hymnbook, among 525 hymns, one is about hell. They dared not omit it entirely. Blake cheerfully showed them the way out of their difficulties: diabolic reading throughout. Where the Bible appears to sanction vengeance, the Elect speak, and these are cautionary tales preserved by the Holy Spirit to warn man of his own beastliness. They were to be read according to the inversion of satire. It is simply a matter of ascertaining the literary genre of a given passage. They were to be read as black instead of white. The procedure places the Bible at the discretion of the individual reader, but Blake was systematic in his interpretation, and firm in his belief that vision would reveal to any man the true nature of God and make clear which passages were black. With a mind like this at work in his poetry, is it any wonder that critics, once the difficulties of reading are surmounted, find it the chief problem to ascertain where to read Blake white and where to read him black? He took the Bible for his model, and his writing flows from contrary to contrary, just as he thought the Bible moved.

---

[19] See Watts's introductory remarks to his Psalm versions, and his notes on Psa 3, 6, 14, 16, 18. Where it was possible, he "endeavoured to turn the edge of them against our spiritual adversaries," but he omitted these Psalms, and such verses as Psa 52:5; 54:5; 59:13; 64:7, 8; 70:2, 3; 79:6; 140:10. In *Reliquiae Juveniles* he published a version of Psa 137, a "noble ode," but unsuited for Christian use because of the prayer for the destruction of Babylon. Watts was not a pacifist (nor were Wesley and Blake). Grandson of a hero of the Navy, he could denounce enemies within the body politic (Psa 58) and write vigorous war songs for what seemed to him a righteous war (Psa 59). Blake thought a righteous war aimed at forgiveness of the Elect, because only energy had power to forgive. Forgiveness was not a passive act, the action of a slave. All *Jerusalem* speaks of the energy of forgiveness, the strength and vision it demands, never an act to be performed by weakness of spirit, nor mere submission, but a positive force moving toward a resolution. It seems to me that Wesley, who thought so too, forgot this in *Hymns for the Nation*, and it is in the light of these generalizations that I call the book excessive and extravagant.

Mrs Nannicantipot said when rebuked, "I don't think it's prophane to say 'Hang Pharaoh'" (443). Blake expands this principle. The Bible has its villains, and the reader must locate them and must determine when a character appears in villainous aspect. Moses sometimes appears in one aspect, sometimes in another. But only a reader of Blake who lacks subtlety can conclude that his message for the world was "Hang Moses." Blake was not an anarchist.

When his reading of the Bible is seen in the light of theological controversies of his day, his reading appears much less erratic. He need only to have read newspapers and popular periodicals to know all he needed to know about the lower and higher criticism. There was, for example, quite a stir made about declaring non-canonical the story of the woman taken in adultery.

The Bible at times makes it clear that the words of the Elect are opposed to right principles. One such place is the line from Wesley used by Donald Davie to illustrate both Wesley's sophistication and his devastating simplicity. Wesley can pierce through the stubborn coatings of generalities that surround the human heart because the minute particulars contain the universal. When one knows the stories, he can pierce as Lear's words pierce, "Pray you, undo this button."

> This man receiveth sinners still.

It can stand alone as a clear call to conversion, can be heard by the simplest. But it does not stand alone. Layer after layer of irony has fallen away to leave that bare simplicity. The words were spoken by the Pharisees in accusation of Jesus in the Temple. He answered, not with denial, but with stories, three immortal stories of the lost sheep, the lost coin, the prodigal son. It is the obvious irony directed against all organized religion that these words could ever constitute an accusation. From this obvious point, irony on irony develops. Jesus did not answer with accusation. The final irony is that the words are true, and are the only hope of the Pharisees as they are the hope of all men.

This reading of Luke 15:2 has become orthodox. But Wesley went beyond "orthodoxy" in his daring use of such ironies. Quite recently I have seen him criticized for an interpretation of Matthew 25:27 in his journal.[20] He used it also in *Short Hymns*, but the critic did not catch him. The words of the Elect which authorized the Crucifixion were, "His blood be on us,

---

[20] Mabel Richmond Brailsford, *A Tale of Two Brothers* (New York 1954) 145.

and on our children." Wesley said it was the greatest prayer a man could speak. This interpretation is not yet "orthodox," and it is proof of Wesley's "divine audacity," but it is only proper to point out that in this reading he was merely paraphrasing his favorite poet, the holy Mr Herbert.[21] Herbert and Wesley could read white for black, and did. The rebel who is rejected by the Elect is that which will save them. The words spoken by the Elect are cruel, but they had spoken better than they knew, and the words are the hope of the world. It is ironic that so much hope can spring from cruelty, such great truths can be spoken by it. But that is the principle of contraries. The very truth and energy of their cruelty is the contrary force that may move them.

I do not compare Blake to Wesley as a religious poet. Blake cannot stand the comparison. Bernard Manning said of the Wesley hymnbook (the 1830 edition with its supplement) that it ranked with the Psalms, the Book of Common Prayer, and the canon of the Mass. "In its own way, it is perfect, unapproachable in its perfection. You cannot alter it except to mar it; it is a work of supreme devotional art by a religious genius." [22] But Blake is comparable in his audacity, his power of memory, the intimacy with which he fuses myth in every moment of life. His ironies have been read, not with too much complexity, but too little. I call attention to the scope of both poets, their sophistication in irony, their ability so to control tone that the same words may carry at one time irony, at another time the most direct and piercing simplicity.

[21] George Herbert, "The Sacrifice," lines 105–112.
[22] Manning, 14.

3 ENTHUSIASM WITHOUT MYSTICISM

CHARLES WESLEY and William Blake have been called mystics, but never during their careers as poets did they call themselves by that name. As young men, the Wesleys were strongly drawn to mysticism, Charles the more strongly of the two. They read widely in mystic writings during their days at Oxford.[1] All Wesley hymn publications, however, came after they had made a complete rejection of mysticism.[2] The preface of their first joint hymnbook is one of the key writings of Methodism. It announced and explained their stand; with a lifelong and reiterated emphasis, they denounced mysticism as an enemy of Christianity compared to which other enemies were trifling.

It is important to remember what they did not reject. They did not abandon their Moravian friends, who were mystics. They said the Catholic mystics were "lights set in dark places," and often had done great good. The writings of mystics were published in inexpensive editions and urged upon the Societies. The first sentence of the famous preface says they had made some use of the mystic method of writing poetry; and, with appropriate changes, they did use it at times in the hymns.[3] The hymns are full of allusions to the

[1] V. H. H. Green, *The Young Mr. Wesley: A Study of John Wesley and Oxford* (New York 1961), *John Wesley* (London 1964). Both books comment on the alteration of opinions and frame of mind; the first book lists the record of Wesley's reading from his unpublished Oxford diaries. No such particular record exists of the reading of Charles Wesley, but there are some records, and his biographers have accumulated conjectures about his reading, to which conjectures Dr Green's work adds valuable basis for additions, considering the close relation between the brothers during these years. I am grateful to Dr Green for answering my questions about these early diaries.

[2] John Wesley published two collections of hymns before he and Charles published their first joint hymnbook, the first being published in April 1737. Five months before, in a letter to his brother Samuel (Nov 23 1736), John Wesley told of his complete break with mysticism. The first joint hymnbook contains the earliest poetry written by Charles Wesley, and therefore the preface covers all his known verse. He wrote verse at Oxford, but none is known to have survived. Dr Baker (257–259) prints the one line of verse known to have been written earlier, and discusses the possible nature of that early verse. Charles Wesley's diary (May 23 1738) records his individual statement on related matters, and I allude to this statement in several of my conclusions about his poetry as a whole.

[3] Both the method and the adaptations of that method by the Wesleys can best be studied in the light of Louis L. Martz, *The Poetry of Meditation* (Yale 1954). I have so studied all Wesley poetry. Certain parts of the method are not appropriate to the hymn genre; but both

writings of those who practiced or sanctioned religious mysticism. We can be very sure that such allusions were not "taints" in the Wesleys' opinion, for they edited the hymns (some of them as many as twelve times) with the avowed purpose of removing any taint of mysticism that may have been overlooked.[4] The Wesleys did not lack sympathy for new friends whose mystical predilections were well known.[5] They themselves saw no visions and heard no voices, but they were interested in reports of mysterious phenomena. Although they found little they could credit, John Wesley investigated the reports with open mind. Samuel Johnson shared this interest, thinking it unwise to circumscribe too narrowly the boundaries of the possible, and he trusted Wesley's judgment in such matters.[6] Blake also read widely in mystical subjects, observed phenomena, used in his writings many allusions to the mystics, accepted what he found good, rejected what was incompatible.

Certainly the Wesleys recognized the universal seeking of men's hearts on which all religions are based and by which all men seek to find significance for human hope and pain. Certainly they did not deny the revealed religion

---

from their own statement and from the poetry itself it is evident that the Wesleys did not reject the method in many of its aspects. The typical method takes as its focus of meditation an object, a doctrine, a scene; but it often uses a narrative as the focus of meditation. The Wesley method, both because of their personal belief and because of the public nature of the hymn, always concentrates upon a narrative, and has as its outcome some relation with society. To sustain these gross generalizations would demand lengthy discussion of some hymns that seem to be obvious exceptions, but I will take my stand on the generalizations as being inclusive. The list of basic readings in the mystic method given by Dr Martz should be compared with Wesley's reading as listed by Dr Green: Francis of Sales, Bellarmine, Rodriguez, Savonarola, Bernard, Juan de Castiniza, Baxter, Bunyan, Hall, the Cambridge Platonists. Donne was familiar reading. For the Methodist Societies, they published Herbert, Bunyan, Thomas à Kempis, William Law, Norris and others.

[4] It is certain that allusions to these authors had no "taint" in Wesley opinion: Other than English writers, Ignatius, Tertullian, Jerome, Aquinas, Plotinus, Augustine, Teresa of Avila, Lactantius, Antoinette Bourignon, Mme Guyon, Adam of St Victoire, and many allusions to the Breviary and medieval hymns.

[5] Désirée Hirst, *Hidden Riches* (London 1964), tells something of John Wesley's association with the mystics, an example being Ralph Mather (240–241). Miss Hirst gives backgrounds and traces the personal relations of the groups of people affected by mystical thought.

[6] Boswell's *Life of Johnson*, ed Hill-Powell (Oxford 1934) III 297–298. Anna Seward expressed amusement both at Johnson's credulity and at his confidence in John Wesley's investigations, and Johnson rebuked her vehemently. One should like to know what Wesley might have made of Blake's visions. It is well known that Johnson complained about how Wesley never had time to let him "have his talk out," but it is not so well known that once Johnson found John Wesley completely at leisure. A year before Johnson died, there was a time when he thought he was on his death-bed and sent for Wesley. There is no record of the conversation other than the brief one in Wesley's journal (Dec 18 1783): "I spent two hours with that great man, Dr Johnson, who is sinking into the grave by a gentle decay."

of Christianity that places trust in the Incarnation as a unique historical act of vicarious suffering, death, and redemption, and in the reality of the Resurrection. Nor were Methodists inveighing against systematic devotions; that is the meaning of the word Methodist. What then?

Neglect of the ordinary means of grace, and substituting for those means of grace a contemplative quietism, abstraction from social and practical Christianity, withdrawal from the world for periods of time in an attempt to induce deliberately a holy frame of mind. These were great dangers, precisely because mysticism can trap the highest minds and the purest spirits in the most deceitful of all natural religions, and can do it by means of the holiest desires. Contemplation slides into self-contemplation. To be sure, it is a sin for a man to pride himself upon his good works; but good works, because they are works, have a way of correcting that pride in sincere hearts when they are performed in sincerity; so patently do the works go astray, so often do they fail, that even this sin is less dangerous than the self-hypnosis by which a man persuades himself that his frame of mind is holy. The deluded man, seeming to achieve his aim, exempts himself from refutation of his "holiness," which, being self-proved, may become impregnable in its self-righteousness.

The Wesleys were not the first to recognize and dread this danger, nor the first to urge the ordinary means of grace as they are practiced in social Christianity to serve as practical insurance against it. But they felt within themselves, and saw around them, cause for special dread of abstraction and its self-righteousness. They emphasized elements always present in Christian thought, but gave to these elements a development that resulted in the Wesleys' unique contribution to the history of theology. The strong force drawing toward mysticism was countered (as I think it was in Blake's case) by a much stronger force. The product was the Wesleys' determination to submit dogma to the test of experience in a belief, both honest and devout, that experience was itself revelation.[7]

One can draw no parallel between the two poets on lines of religious discipline; any likeness must lie elsewhere. The Wesley preface says, "The Gospel of Christ knows of no religion, but social; no holiness, but social holiness"

[7] George Croft Cell, *The Rediscovery of John Wesley* (New York 1935) 94–129, 360 ff, gives a systematic study of mysticism and empiricism, and throughout the book a description of the relation of Wesley theology to contemporary thought and to the history of Christian theology which has been of great value to me, and agrees with opinions formed from my own reading. I should more properly say that I agree with Professor Cell's conclusions; he might not agree with mine, which were arrived at in other ways and with other purposes, and are stated in other terms.

(ɪ xxii). In clear contrast, Blake's message "To the Christians" says, "I know of no other Christianity and of no other Gospel than the liberty both of body & mind to exercise the Divine Arts of the Imagination" (229–230). His Christianity has no institutional aspect at all. All his life, he neglected those "means of grace" to which the Wesleys refer most often; record indicates that he never took communion or attended religious services other than his own christening, wedding, and burial.

Wesley writings on the subject echo with Paul's words to the Thessalonians: build one another up, esteem one another in love for the work's sake, quench not the Spirit, despise not prophesyings, prove all things, know them which labor among you, build up.

Blake's message closes, "Let every Christian, as much as in him lies engage himself openly & publicly before all the World in some Mental pursuit for the Building up of Jerusalem." The similarity lies not chiefly in the Pauline vocabulary and phrasing, but in the fact that both messages are open, public, aimed at edification of the community, urging all Christians to work vigorously in the public eye for the public good. If Blake's is only a "religion of art," it differs from typical examples of such religions in that it has no smell of decadence, self-conscious eccentricity, or sterile aloofness. Loathing inertia and abstraction, he kept his hands busy about the means of grace as he defined them.

There were and are men who are mad, visionaries, enthusiasts, and mystics, but the terms are not synonymous. Christopher Smart, at times in his life, was all four things at once. But a man may be, like Yeats, only a visionary. Or, like Donne and Herbert, only mystics. Or, like Charles Wesley, only an enthusiast. Blake was an enthusiast and a visionary. Modern psychiatrists, even with all their reasons for distrusting "visions," say that madness must be measured by other yardsticks than the mere seeing of visions, the first question to ask being: Does the person function normally? So far as is known, there was no hour in the lives of Blake or the Wesleys when they were not functioning normally. Blake's visions in no way inconvenienced the day's work, but were simply part of the day's work. His wife once went so far as to remind a guest that it is better if an artist is allowed to give his attention to his sitter. Blake on that occasion may have been a bit ruffled, but even so he managed some small talk while producing two magnificent portraits of his sitter (the ghost of a flea).

Insanity was one of ten popular accusations against Wesley enthusiasm, the other nine being: alliance with Roman Catholicism, alliance with the Jacobites, tendency to schism, pressure toward a renewal of the religious wars of the preceding century, antinomianism, arrogance, hypocrisy, vulgarity, excess. Surely at this date it is not necesary to take them up seriatim. Does anyone now think John Wesley was a secret emissary of the Pope or was in person the Young Pretender? It was often said that he was one or both, and I think it can be proved that he was not. During the American Revolution and especially during the time of the Gordon Riots the charges reached a peak of intensity (Wesley property was listed for burning during the anti-Catholic riots). Since Charles Wesley was human, the intensity of the attacks may account for his lapses in *Hymns for the Nation* which give grounds for some of these charges. For all the charges cannot be so lightly dismissed as the statement that John Wesley was the Young Pretender.

With both terms, mysticism and enthusiasm, I begin with theological definitions of the word grace, and (warily) attempt to apply certain elements of the definitions to Blake in terms that are non-theological, but which demonstrate similarities between the two poets that seem to place them in similar positions with respect to contemporary controversies. For this purpose, *The Doctrine of Grace* by Bishop Warburton is peculiarly useful. It was a personal attack on John Wesley as the fountainhead of enthusiasm, written by a prince of the church who has gone down in history as a foe of deism. It concentrates on the definition of grace. Since poetry rather than theology is my subject, Warburton's treatise is most valuable because it deals extensively with language theory as it relates to the doctrine of grace.[8]

As Blake knew well, the importance of deism lay in its power to modify Christian doctrine. Deism in its pure form never had many subscribers. Strict deist dogma, as accepted by Matthew Tindal, for example, held that a rational deity had created man with sufficient reason to discern natural law, and then had withdrawn from human affairs because no further intervention was necessary; human nature was static and uniform and had altered in no significant way since creation; the Incarnation and Redemption added nothing to natural law; the Crucifixion was therefore unnecessary, and the Christian religion, being superfluous, was a violation of logical economy.

---

[8] *The Doctrine of Grace* (1763), Warburton's *Works*, ed Richard Hurd, 12 vols (1811) VII 237–455. Both Wesley and Whitefield answered publicly: George Whitefield, *Observations on Some Fatal Mistakes in a Book Lately Published etc*; Wesley's published letter is in his *Works*, 17 vols (1812) XIII 262–326. Thomas Leland of Dublin challenged the language theory, Hurd answered Leland, and Leland (1765) answered again. John Wesley made another private response (*Journal* IV 539). Warburton sent the manuscript to him, asking to be shown "wherein he had erred." Wesley (the man whose biographers say had no sense of humor) corrected errors in Latin, Greek and Hebrew quotations, corrected the readings in standard glosses, and returned the manuscript for publication with no other comment. He did remark to his brother that he had not thought the Bishop to be so poor a scholar — he seemed hardly to know the Greek Testament at all.

The most efficacious eighteenth-century version of Occam's razor was not deism, but semi-deism. Warburton states the logical economy of semi-deism. Churchmen in general, caught between deism and enthusiasm, attempted to answer both enemies at once by protesting that the Church was as logical as anybody; taking on deistic ideas and vocabulary, they proved in the face of the Book of Common Prayer that human nature was static and God was, by now at least, *dégagé*. Warburton had no desire to prove the Christian religion completely unnecessary. He set the date of God's withdrawal from human intercourse at the completion of the scriptural canon. Thus he kept Christianity in the scheme of things, and kept the Bible inspired. But inspired only just so far.

Language, he said, is made up of *single terms* and *phrases and idioms*. Only the single terms of the Bible (names, actions, abstractions) were divinely inspired and had universal significance. Phrases and idioms result from "local barbarities," not from divine inspiration. Eloquence lies in these local barbarities, in these transient elements of language. Eloquence stifles reason and beclouds the significance of the single terms. It enflames the passions, and reason can never be vigorously exerted in the presence of passion. Eloquence, therefore, must not be used in the preaching of the Gospel. The Church was "perfectly established." The Christian life was attended with "ease and honour." Reason alone would urge any man into the Kingdom by personal self-interest. Reason was sufficient both to propound and to perceive the truth of the Gospel. This is the correct doctrine of grace.

Language had evolved in the direction of the abstract as man became more civilized. Metaphor is a primitive and faulty means of communication. The use of any figurative language whatsoever in the pulpit is "deceitful and vicious." At all times in serious discourse, but most religiously when in the pulpit, a man should confine discourse to single terms, avoiding the barbarities of eloquence and employing only those words which have precise and rational meaning.

Warburton makes sharp distinction between art and serious discourse. He was a friend of Pope and Garrick, and had no objection to figurative language, physical gesture, cadencing of voice so long as they were confined to art. But in "serious discourse," they were inappropriate — "deceitful and vicious" — and he adds the full weight of theology in denouncing their use in the pulpit. He anticipates an idea of the associational psychologists, who spoke of physical gesture and cadencing of voice as if they were equivalents of figurative language. He called Wesley "an actor," "a mere actor," "a paltry mimic." Audiences did at times compare Wesley to Garrick; Wesley voices were tireless, rich and varied in tone, of almost unbelievable carrying power and clarity, and provably effective in appeal to emotions. The great voice was, of course, Whitefield's; he was the only man Garrick ever called a greater actor than himself — but the Wesley voices were eloquent.

Warburton reasons thus: appeal to emotion is dishonest because superfluous, emotion being a superfluity in religion. Appeal to the Holy Spirit is excessive, for it is presumptuous to say that man had need at that date of further assistance of the Spirit to make the Gospel clear and effective. To postulate the possibility of divine intervention into human hearts and to speak as if the law of reason had not been established gave proof of fanaticism. Insistence on need for social change or personal "conversion" was vulgar. Civilized men in a civilized sociey had proof of the value of Christianity. "The weight of human testimony and the conclusions of human reason afford abundant conviction to support us in perseverance." It was perseverance he wanted, not change. The Christian religion was "perfectly established." The Christian life was attended with "ease and honour." The abjuring of metaphor was the very mark of the civilized man. His entire appeal is to good taste, decorum, and the preservation of the *status quo*.

Distrust of art as something uncontrollable, fear of the theatre, fear of metaphor as an irrational and suspect means of communication, are by no means restricted to the Age of Reason, but can be found in Plato and the Puritans. The Puritans argued that it was a historical fact that the people of God had no theatre. The Puritan plain style also abjured metaphor. The New Testament uses none, none being needed once the revelation was complete and "plain." The parables are similitudes; metaphors are lies. Bunyan argues the point in the preface to *The Pilgrim's Progress*. He anticipates and answers criticism; his book may be called "dark," "feigned," lacking in "solidness," because "Metaphors make us blind." He answers that he has used no metaphor. This morning's paper reports that Dr Roy Lee, in a sermon based on the writings of the Bishop of Woolrich, said, "The thesis that religious metaphors have become harmful in the Christian church is not considered revolutionary in English theological circles." No indeed. Nor is it reversionary. It is a constant. But in different ages, the arguments are differently stated. Fear of the unknown, fear of being "blind" in the "dark," asks reassurance of Bunyan and of Warburton, just as the fear of change that accompanies science asks for reassurance. It is the duty of an Establishment to reassure. Warburton does appear to be taking his ease in Zion and saying to John Wesley, "I'm all right, Jack," in tones typical of his day; but he draws on old strengths for his arguments, and it is perhaps more fair to him to say his message is, "You're all right, Jack." Calm yourself.

Warburton's modification of deism was one interpretation of empiricism. The position of the evangelicals was equally an outgrowth of empiricism. The change which they called conversion, the New Birth, was necessary in the experience of all men, because the Word, although It had independent existence, was for no man a living reality until It was realized in personal experience. Like Warburton, they drew on old beliefs. Like him, they addressed themselves to present needs. Answers to Warburton emphasized the collects, invocation, benediction, order of baptism, and offices of his own service, saying that it seemed at the very least inhospitable to invite the presence of the Spirit at every authorized service on the proviso that He make no remarks and suggest no changes. But — give or take a few adjectives — what Warburton and Bishop Butler said about Wesley was true — with one very important exception. The enthusiasts were as strong in their appeal to "common sense" as the deists; they claimed no special power for themselves, but rather said that all men were subject to the threat or the promise of the visitations of the Spirit, which came by ordinary means of grace and represented the "common sense" of the Christian life.

Warburton did not mention the hymns. Indeed, all the lampoons, burlesques, serious and satiric attacks left the Methodist hymns almost unscathed. This was no compliment; quite the contrary. It was an age that took poetry with so little seriousness that it never occurred to Warburton or Samuel Foote that the real dynamite was where histories of the movement have located it, in the hymnbook. Had Warburton wanted examples of just what he was denouncing, he could have found none better than the hymns of Charles Wesley. If examples are wanted today, there still are none better. Wesley's masterful handling of cadence left hardly a false tone or accent in his collected works. His ear was exquisite and quick and his memory for tone was retentive in the extreme. The effect of his work on emotions is a matter of history. Frankly theatrical gestures are written into the verb structure with an implicit kinesthesia that impels toward physical action. Stage effects and light cues are written into the text. Wesley tunes are emphatically theatrical. Friends in the theatre, like J. F. Lampe, a convert from deism, helped to keep them so. The hymns arise from and invoke the intervention of the Spirit in common affairs, sometimes as by incantation, sometimes as bluntly as, "Talk with me, Lord." Metaphor blends the day's work with another world almost by punning, so closely are two meanings folded into a single sound.

The dark satanic mills of Newcastle lit the night sky, and the workers sang:

> See how great a flame aspires
> Kindled by a spark of grace.

Stoneworkers sang:

> Strike with the hammer of Thy word,
> And break these hearts of stone.

Staffordshire miners, with voices purer than the Cornish, sweeter even than the Welsh, in Wesley ears, deep in the shafts sang:

> Lift up your eyes, ye sons of light
> Triumphant.

Cornish fishermen, who taught their children to fancy that they, too, could remember Wesley, sang:

> Teach me to cast my nets aright.

Farmers sang:

> Look on the fields and see them white,
> Already white to harvest see.
> Moved by the Spirit's softest wind,
> The sinners to their Saviour turn.
> Their hearts are all as one inclined:
> Their hearts are bowed as waving corn.

Dozens of songs spoke of the work of soldiers, dozens told of the sailor's life, hundreds told of the shepherd's work. There were songs for teachers and masons and students, for all who cook and clean and build and fight, but none exclusively theirs, for all metaphor came from a single myth. The prayer of all who thus built together was:

> Son of the carpenter, receive
> This humble work of mine.

There were thousands of variations on eating and drinking and the paying of visits — those acts of Communion and the Visitation of the Spirit.

> If still Thou dost with sinners eat,
> Come, dearest Lord, and quickly come.

Verbs are active, imperative, urgent. Talk, see, strike, break, lift, teach, look, receive, come. And quickly come — into this moment and make me know it is the very mercy of eternity, make fruitful man's sense of time moment by moment. For nothing but the active Word can fully explain the day's work; only the day's work can fully activate the Word in human life.

It is tendentious thus to place Blake's words in Wesley's mouth, the more culpable because I do not agree with Warburton that poetry is not serious discourse, nor with Auden that "poetry makes nothing happen," nor with those who say philosophers leave the world as they find it. Locke did not leave the world as he found it. Charles Wesley's poetry made many things happen. It is the more culpable because, while insisting upon the social, political, and theological importance of this poetry, I do not place Blake as being in complete agreement with those principles. From Blake's writings of all his life there can be accumulated many caustic retorts to the point of view represented by Warburton,[9] but it would be misleading to cite them as if his answer was identical with John Wesley's answer. Wesley's fearlessness was the contrary of Warburton's timidity, not its negation. Wesley and the bishops argued as members of an Establishment argue, Warburton choosing Wesley rather than Whitefield as his opponent because Wesley was a member of the Establishment, and arguing publicly on a matter of public concern.

I have conscientiously given account of the two extreme ideas of Blake's relation to Wesley; some readers of Blake see him as Wesley's fellow in anarchy; some see him as utterly opposed to the discipline Wesley represented. These hymns give the crux of Wesley discipline, the basis of all discipline. They are, on one hand, the voice of the Establishment, a much more

---

[9] Blake's marginalia on Bishop Watson's *Apology* are applicable. Even Paine, said Blake, deist though he was, never denied "That God does & always did converse with honest Men" (604).

"William Cowper Esq[re]":
And tis most wicked in a Christian Nation
For any Man to pretend to Inspiration. (498)

What is a Church? & What
Is a Theatre? are they Two & not One? can they Exist Separate? (205)

The relation of the Wesleys to the Church of England is a complex matter. It is true, and it is to his credit, that Palamabron-Wesley worked within the social order, to his credit that he loyally loved the Church and would not leave it even under provocation. It is also true (and to his credit) that Bishop Butler did not have Wesley thrown out, also under considerable provocation. If I understand the *jus ubique docendi*, Butler had the right to do so, and I think Butler had the power; he was a much more powerful man than Warburton. The bishops needed Wesley, and he needed them. He said in his old age, "It seems the scandal of the Cross is ceased. I have become, I know not how, an honourable man." That is a joke; the last thing a prophet should desire is that the scandal should cease. It is a joke, a deep saying, one Blake would have understood. Should "ease and honour" ever attend the Christian life? Had he compromised the Gospel in giving soft answers to bishops? It did seem at that moment (and Wesley made no secret of his pleasure in it) that the contraries had met in mutual forgiveness.

insidious sustaining of Church and State than Warburton's voice. Historians have said this voice held England back from revolution in an Age of Revolution — in the sermons, yes, but more effectively in the hymns. The hymns were in the mouths of the people, encouraging "tyranny" by their preaching of "contentment," and by their preaching of the presence of the Spirit in mills and mines and all that is dark and satanic in human life. On the other hand, this is the discipline that taught thousands to read and write and be clean and work steadily and save money, placing in thousands of hands the instruments of social change. Inasmuch as Warburton opposed social change, it is the voice of his Enemy. Inasmuch as Blake opposed all discipline, it is the voice of his Enemy; and those who read Blake in this manner must of necessity read "The Chimney Sweeper" as satire. That is a genuine Methodist angel who speaks. It is a genuine Methodist response to the angel to conclude that Tom Dacre, even in the situation he is in, will in some way be kept safe by doing his duty to his heavenly Father, safe, and even happy, even warm. Charles Wesley's hymns, heard thus, are the effective voice of Blake's Enemy, cadenced, singing, dramatic, active, giving to the masses their own voice in emotional and imaginative power. And, to the degree that Warburton feared these very qualities, the hymns are his true Enemy.

Wesley and Blake are comparable in their arrogance, vulgarity, and excess. These traits of enthusiasm entered into all their poetic successes and can be seen with greatest clarity in their poetic failures. It is arrogant to keep on saying, "Mark well my words! they are of your eternal salvation," when nobody told you to say it. Their nationalistic arrogance, if that is what we must call it, was inescapable; if anything was to be accomplished by their message (and they thought something might be) and if their work was to accomplish it (and they thought they had to try) then it must be done now and in England because England was where they were, and it is the here and now that matters.

There is something vulgar and excessive about the very desire to become all things to all men. Blake had some interesting conversations with Ezekiel about the odd things this prophetic impulse involved a man in. Wesley and Blake were a bit noisy, sometimes a little shrill, unresigned to sit in mystic meditation waiting for the millennium, not conforming in that large conformity by which most men lead lives of quiet desperation. The names of their common enemies were quietism and despair, the despair of abstraction and the quietism of mystics. The mystics advised the Wesleys to remember that God had said, "Be still and know that I am God." So He did, they answered, as always setting the words within their own narrative. He said so not once but twice, both times when He was urging His people to march forward with all their might, and sing praises as they marched and moved and fought.

Blake, like Wesley, was unable to think of anything in terms other than religious. "Are not Religion & Politics the Same Thing?" (205) "As the true method of knowledge is experiment the true faculty of knowing must be the faculty which experiences. This faculty I treat of . . . Poetic Genius" (2). The two statements span the years of his entire engraved canon. His use of the word science shows that he wanted the findings of experiment to be viewed with eyes that refused to see only generalities. His books as they lie in the hand are products of exacting science. He opposed not science but the abstraction of knowledge, and he betook himself outside the orthodoxies of religion and science because the forms available to him seemed to be rooted in abstract thought. In his prophetic books, he describes a state of existence that sounds like hell. In this state, the creatures of his imagination out-howl the creatures of Cotton Mather's imagination in their flames. It is not a final state, but an experience through which men pass to an experienced heaven. These descriptions have both theological and scientific aspects. The inflexible amalgam of Puritanism and deism received in the nineteenth century a profound shock from the theory of evolution, and an amalgam of these traits can still muster opposition; at one level, the theory is contrary to God's word; at the level of satiric cartoons, the theory is presented as opposed to good taste, it being vulgar to suggest that man ever underwent any profound change. Blake's story of creation opposed the deist stasis with a violence that shoved him beyond any orthodox account of creation. God, he said, had not created man a static thing, but rather had created the already fallen man *for* experience, so that in the mercy of eternity man might undergo the salvation of experience. This view is as far from any passive purgatory as it is from deism. Recent work of Carmen Kreiter indicates that Blake incorporated into his description of this state of man such theories of evolution as came to his notice and possibly even so scientific a procedure as open-heart surgery.[10]

Milton in his prophetic office gloriously solved the problems of vulgarity and excess. He was a greater poet than Wesley or Blake, but in all fairness to the enthusiasts it must be said that he did not have their problems. Much had changed since Milton wrote; Locke, Defoe, Swift, Fielding, Hogarth

[10] Carmen S. Kreiter, "Evolution and William Blake," *Studies in Romanticism* IV (Winter 1965) 110–118.

had lived and worked. For his poetic purposes, Milton could ignore findings of science that were well known to him. Wesley and Blake had to submit a complete report. Milton could omit much. Wesley and Blake had to write about "the screech of Childbirth" and the "groans Of Death" (175). They did not always write well, but they were heirs of empiricism. Locke must be answered, if at all, in Lockean terms. Honesty demanded of them a sort of involvement in human experience that Milton could avoid. Milton drew Cromwell's counsellors in diabolic manner. Blake's Schofield is less impressive, vulgar, but necessary. Belial represents evil. Blake, in the most exalted context, reminds his reader that he meant Schofield.

Milton kept even the screech of childbirth of his two great grotesques, Sin and Death, within the dynamic principle of decorum. The strange births recorded by Blake are excessive. It is good to know that he had some precedent in Indian creation legends,[11] but it makes his poetry seem more excessive, not less, when one sees how quiet and orderly the legends are compared to all that sprouting of off-spring at every joint and organ that goes on in his poetry.[12] That business about births from "conglobing" blood always made me faintly sick; when I found out that Blake was talking about bits and pieces of bodies and embryological specimens, I congratulated myself on being a sensitive reader, for that is how I feel about embryological specimens, and more than ever, I admired Blake's power of conveying emotional realism, but it is not decorous writing, nor is his out-house humor decorous.

So precisely ordered a universe as Milton's would not do for Blake. Blake gets his universe in a mess. There are stretches of poetry where he labors as if sight and hearing were impaired, struggling like a man half deaf and half blind. Things must shriek and bang on forges in order to make themselves heard, must fall flaming from star to star in order to make themselves seen. Compare the sound effects of *Paradise Lost* Book II with the racket set up at these places by Blake's abstractions (and at these places, they are abstractions, and that, too, is necessary). It must have cost gargantuan labor to bring the verse under perfect control at the end of *Jerusalem*, to make it a splendor to the eyes and ears. The struggles that are seen and felt throughout *Jerusalem* are necessary to the poem. Part of the story of man is this risk of artistic failure. Blake takes every risk, and it is exciting, but it is not always

[11] Piloo Nanavutty, "William Blake and Hindu Creation Myths," *The Divine Vision* (London 1957) 180.

[12] The myths give examples of such strange births, and Blake may have read them; but there is nothing in them so extravagant as his creatures, born from bosom, loins, heart, head, throat, breath, hair, brains, back, nostrils, feet. "Conglobing" is Milton's word, used in describing creation, but as the word appears in *Paradise Lost* it does not grate on the sensibilities.

suave. One comes to accept all of Wesley and all of Blake in a way one never quite accepts the early Keats or the late Wordsworth. Everything seems necessary.

All the real poets I know can quote golden treasuries of bad verse and do so with joy. By the same token, musicians and musicologists worth their salt take joy in bad music. When this trait occurs in conjunction with the acceptance of all of Wesley as necessary, the result is a shameless glorying in the horrid history of Wesley tunes. Dr Austin Lovelace, who can sing them, tells me they have never been sung in America and that no effort is made to use them in the new edition of the Methodist hymnal. The tunes are vulgar (beneath our contempt) or excessive (over our heads). Around the Wesley house, Bach was spoken of as The Man. His two sons were infant prodigies and his grandson, named Sebastian, was also a brilliant performer and composer. Charles and John Wesley loved the florid, difficult music of Purcell and Handel (Handel set three Wesley hymns), but they had low friends and a deplorable love of music. Any kind. Wesley tunes came from modern opera, popular stage shows, Handel's *Susanna*, Bickerstaffe's *Love in a Village*, Carey's song in praise of the taking of Portobello by Admiral Vernon, Arne's *Eliza*, and jigs. "Love Divine," that mixture of pure doctrine and sexuality which for decades was the wedding hymn of Methodism, is a parody of the curtain song from the Restoration equivalent of our musical show *Camelot*. It was sung by Venus (no less) at the close of Dryden's *King Arthur*, set by Purcell. The Wesleys used Purcell's tune, and the opening lines are frank parody. I commend it to all who find Wesley deficient in doctrinal statement and to any who want to investigate his method of Biblical allusion. It is a far better lyric than Dryden's. The trail of Wesley tunes would lead one today from Lincoln Center to City Center, from Broadway to Tin Pan Alley, from the Rare Book Room of Union Theological Seminary to some very red lights indeed. Polite Methodists hang their heads at the name of Nancy Dawson; it seems impossible that Charles Wesley could have written it. He wrote it, and he liked it, and published it, and published a revised and expanded version. It is not a very good song.

A gang of drunken military men tried to break up an outdoor meeting he was holding by singing the "lewd" song of Nancy Dawson, who was (as best Dr Baker has been able to make out in his pursuit of the elusive Nancy) keeper of a bawdy house.[13] Wesley did not call the cops or disband the meeting; the Wesleys never did. His quick ear caught the tune, he improvised

---

[13] Baker 117.

his own words full of puns on military life, taught them to the crowd, and the mob was quelled. Dr Baker has not been able to discover whether the mob left in defeat or remained to sing the Wesley version. This is the sort of thing one wants to know about Wesley. Among the Dionysians, did he find an Areopagite?

He invented a myth and attached it to his already-existing myth, a story of chivalric love and high emprise. Once there was a beautiful lady named not Nancy but Music. She, like you, good soldiers, was listed (enlisted) and pressed (impressed) against her will into a life that was contrary to her true nature. Shall we rescue her? His "Nancy Dawson" is a comprehensive offer to reclaim all music for "the Great Lover," to make song in its entirety into a love song for Him, no matter how "Drunken or lewd or light the lay." His meter and alliterations lilt with the cheap hornpipe tune.[14]

Now, this is what is wrong with enthusiasm. In words that would have seemed excessive to Bishop Warburton, Wesley had prayed that God would "with jealous care" arm him "To serve the present age." He had in mind Paul's magnificent arming in Ephesians. He wanted the sword of the Spirit which is the preparation of the gospel of peace.

Having prayed, he goes on his way and produces this parody — surely a lower form of swordsmanship than Cyrano's extempore thrust and parry.

This is the risk a poet runs when he fuses his life with both protagonists of the story of the woman taken in adultery and comes to think that everything that lives is holy, and one must therefore behave in a practical manner according to an empirical philosophy, believing in the supreme importance of experience, exalting common sense to the Elysian Fields of metaphysics. Paul did not mention in his panoply the quality of good nature and the knack of writing verse under any circumstances, but on this occasion they served the present age. Wesley did not ride his circuits quite unarmed.

Yeats, working from a comprehensive and all-explaining myth, miraculously could make his family and friends into mythic figures without sacrificing their humanity; could, in perfectly lucid verse, make a solar myth of Major Gregory and leave him Robert Gregory still; could write a "Prayer

---

[14] Listed into the cause of sin
   Why should a good be evil?
Music, alas, too long has been
   Pressed to obey the devil:
Drunken or lewd or light the lay
   Flowed to the soul's undoing,
Widened and strewn with flowers the way
   Down to eternal ruin.

Who on the part of God will rise,
   Innocent sound recover?
Fly on the prey and take the prize,
   Plunder the carnal lover?
Strip him of every moving strain,
   Every melting measure,
Music in virtue's cause retain,
   Rescue the holy pleasure? (v 397)

for My Daughter" that explained the universe and kept the baby still with us. Milton's late espoused saint and Lycidas are not real as is Yeats's Dying Lady, and were not meant to be. Wesley and Blake achieved no such miracles as Yeats along that line, but they had to face similar problems. They had to take the risk of writing about the baby in its cradle, about the fact and act of birth and death. Enthusiasts are beset by excess and vulgarity, facing at all times the threat of all that attends upon reading one's own diary *sub specie aeternitatis*. John Wesley, that remarkable man, balanced (or compassed) both extremes in few words: "Cleanliness is next to godliness." Where the enthusiasts succeed, they give us more alluring heavens than *Paradise Lost* Book III. They involve us deeply in their battles and their dramas of forgiveness. Their failures are conspicuous, their successes are spendid, their risks are all necessary.

4   *SHORT HYMNS* AND *JERUSALEM*

FOR A TIME in 1762 an illness incapacitated Charles Wesley for active ministerial duties. While he was resting, he wrote 5,000 hymns, published that year and reissued in abridged form in 1790. When Osborn printed *Short Hymns on Select Passages of the Holy Scripture*, he incorporated 100 hymns left in manuscript, making 1,509 hymns on the Old Testament and 3,491 on the New Testament, five of the thirteen volumes of the Osborn edition. He worked from John Wesley's personal copy and printed the marginalia. The book is a gloss on the Bible, having no formal organization other than to follow the Scripture, dependent on it, often omitting even the key words when they are prominent in the primary text. The hymns range from versified exposition to Wesley's most exalted lyricism, with useful hymns enough to give a decent level of utility, and some very fine congregational songs, among them "A Charge To Keep." The sections on Genesis and Matthew are models of didactic clarity, collating incidents, objects, and characters from all parts of the Bible and assigning their doctrinal significance in Christian symbolism.

Blake also in mature years restudied the Bible and its relation to life as he knew it. His epic, *Jerusalem*, was the result. It was while studying *Short Hymns* that I first began to write myself notes saying, "Sounds like Blake." The two books are demanding. They demand to be considered in their totality, not in disparate parts. They demand to be read with the imagination. And they reward the reader with the same sort of excitement. Unexpectedly, they turn out to be a couple of cliff-hangers — the appelation being the more apt because hanging on cliffs is a reiterated image in both. Wesley sometimes compounds cliff-hanging with hairbreadth escapes by hanging over cliffs by the hair. They are books of repelling length, breadth of scope, height of purpose. These dimensions of art must be redeemed, as Blake said all dimensions in space and time must be redeemed. Two golden strings are offered as clues. One is the Bible. Wesley's "simplicity," even when set properly beside the text upon which it comments, will work the reader hard in the following of his line of thought. In dealing with any particular text, he works by allusion. Blake marks the text of *Jerusalem* with strange names and places and turns of phrase. These may seem inexplicable, or may be dismissed as some mere *façon de parler* until one makes the necessary association with the passage from the Bible that is alluded to. The second clue is a message from the two poets which says: "Trust the suggestiveness of my disciplined imagination. I stand squarely behind every allusion. All I seem to hint at, I mean. Move with me as emotion and imagination move."

The two books differ in structure, theme, and poetic surface; but, under the pressure of honest reporting on the complexities of human experience, the two theologies and theodicies take on aspects of similarity. As I have said before, I say once again that the similarities may lie outside the boundaries of esthetic judgment and be likenesses of humaneness, of reckless courage, of the largeness of the risks taken. It is a characteristic of the Elect that they do not dare to question their own rightness, dare not ask questions that may have no answers; Wesley and Blake, in mature life, waive their own definitions of their own election and ask the terrible question, "And what if I have been wrong all the time?"

Under this pressure, the two styles are forced to the extreme position of their dissimilarities. Blake, calling upon his countrymen to listen, risks complete failure of communication at the point in his canon when he needed most to make himself heard. His style becomes so cryptic and so concentrated that the common reader can read the history of man only with difficulty. Wesley's poetry almost wrecks itself on his stubborn commitment to clarity. Denied the bolting-holes of obscurity, mixed metaphor, conceit, mysticism, and abstraction, he is hard put to it to render an honest report on his experience with a Reality that comprehends within itself all paradox, all symbol, all counter-symbol. An unpronounceable Charybdis threatens Blake. Wesley dares the Scylla of silliness.

They dare everything. These are ruthless and reckless books. Long ago Wesley and Blake had marked out the territory of the enemy and labeled certain areas: Danger. In these books, they abandon their positions and abandon those barricades they had built for themselves. Leaving their own hard-won certitudes, they make reconnaisance into enemy territory in a manner so reckless that their staunchest friends may well wonder if they have gone over to the enemy. Eventually they fight their way back. Blake was enslaved by no man's system; Wesley made it home to the good old doctrine, but not before both had laid themselves liable to all they most hated and dreaded. Men conscious of their strength will place freedom in jeopardy in order to test and preserve freedom; the hall mark of Wesley and Blake had been freedom from self-conscious moroseness and morbidity. This ultimate value is put in jeopardy by these two books, and one feels that our two heroes are saved by a hair's breadth.[1]

Blake in the opening words of *Jerusalem* says he is perhaps the most sinful of men. He meant it. It was William Blake speaking, not Tartuffe. He assumes all the things he saw as sin, proves them his, incarnates his epic within them, gives his poetry its body by means of them. Under any other circumstances, the ending of the epic in "mutual forgiveness" would be false. He thought Despair and the inculcation of despair the archetype of all sin, and he took upon himself in *Jerusalem* all the ancient forms of despair. The action of his epic is the imposition of an inflexible will upon its opponent, who is threatened with an eternal hell — the archetypal action of despair. The action is accompanied by a hideous battle of the sexes which, if read as any sort of realism or allegory, invites a serious misreading of Blake. The pictures of "Law" and "Love" are terrible in themselves, and represent a terrible

[1] It has been said of Charles Wesley that no one ever wrote at length upon religious experience with less self-consciousness than he. My initial reaction to *Short Hymns* was shock; he turns abruptly from Job and Daniel to consider personal problems in a way that is at first reading as unpleasant as it is uncharacteristic of him; one has a sense of claustrophobia, the last thing one expects from his pages, usually so open, so full of fresh air. *Jerusalem* also is a shocking book. The poetry lapses from any ordinary standard of suavity and decorum, although, on the whole, it represents a great advance in poetic control over *The Four Zoas*. These "failures" arise from the attempt to set in artistic order a much greater emotional intensity and psychological force. Of more importance than these passages, however, is the plot. Blake's stories are not to be ignored. Any -ism or -ology of his must be derived with reference to plot. In *Jerusalem* the conflict with "the female will" (a theme he had dealt with in many earlier works) enters into the action in such a way as to risk the reader's initial impression of a highly concentrated and intensified morbidity. The creation of woman was an act of violence. She came, not in a garden to be man's helpmate, but as the fatal violation of man's integrity. What is wrong with woman was wrong from the first, her insistence upon a life of her own and a will of her own, and her very separate existence is the primal "wrong" in sexual relations. The poem expresses extreme horror of woman's physical presence, her female softness, the cadence of her songs, her tears, her milk, her beauty. This horror reaches a climax in the account of her creation of her own womb, not necessary in the birth process, but necessary for her power to contain man always as an infant, so as to save herself from annihilation, so that the female will may mount the throne of God.

Yes, both books do settle into place. One knows — really knows and feels — what they are doing, that this "female" is universal within both sexes, that it is neither a battle between "real" beings nor allegory, either of which readings would be wrong. But in the meantime, Wesley and Blake have risked your finding them, by one reading, morbid, and by the other reading, generalizing. It is generalization itself that Blake calls feminine, and he associates the quality with Locke, Arthur, Newton, Bacon. His "generalized" picture of family life is a wake, a funeral, a ceremony celebrating the death of the imagination, an apotheosis of the generalized self-righteousness of the family. The generalized picture of sex is a description that covers all pornography: "a sexual Machine, an Aged Virgin." But the Universal Family (*Jerusalem* 27, p 170), and the "minute particular" which contains the universal (that grain of sand in Lambeth, p 181; the resting place of the Bride, p 194; and perhaps that gate, p 179) are not dehumanized, uncreative, empty of all delight. The sound of these passages forms a contrast to the raucous evil.

artistic risk of being falsely construed. Wesley and Blake work always from different definitions of law and love, and resolve by different means these two elements in the paradox of human life. The two books in question state their different views in extreme form; at no point in all their writings are they farther apart. They are alike, however, in the principle of contraries which sets the two elements of that paradox within a state of ceaseless motion.

The orthodox Christian view is to accept both elements of the paradox of law and love. The gnostic position is always revulsion against both elements.[2] Blake used in *Jerusalem* so high a concentration of "orthodox" vocabulary that he has been accused of selling out to orthodox Christianity; and the "action" of *Jerusalem* might be viewed as an "orthodox" punitive action. He used in *Jerusalem* also so high a concentration of gnostic elements, including the gnostic hatred of the flesh and the hatred of law, that he has also been said to have adopted gnostic views. In answering these arguments, one can always go outside the poem and cite *The Everlasting Gospel*, a poem which he finished after *Jerusalem* was completed, and which gives a clear statement of his position. He denied in that last poem the orthodox Christian beliefs, and it is a vigorous anti-gnostic statement.[3] But in *Jerusalem* he presents both systems of thought as aspects of human despair. One must admit, however, that throughout the epic, he teeters on the brink of that obscurantism which is always a part of gnostic thought and practice.

Wesley, in his statements on the pure simplicity of that paradox, teeters on the brink of "Roses are red, Violets are blue, Sugar is sweet, etc." And

[2] Gnostic teaching arose in the first century of the Christian era when precise mathematical computation and the reading of prophecy as historical allegory led people to predict the Second Coming of Christ, and that event did not occur according to their schedule. The result was pessimism amounting to despair. The *gnosis* was the explanation of this failure. To the gnostic, the gospel is not a message openly proclaimed to all, but a secret knowledge mysteriously imparted to an Elect. It was the gnostic explanation of why their calculations miscarried. The gnostic heresy has to do with the interpretation of the nature of Jesus; the gnostics did not deny that he was God, they denied that he was ever made flesh. Characteristic of all forms of gnosticism is revulsion against the flesh; flesh being totally evil, it could not contain the Logos. Gnosticism in all its forms does not always actually encourage immorality; this trait is not a constant. What is a constant is antinomianism toward ethical matters; actions committed in the flesh have no moral or ethical significance, and there can be no Law that governs those actions. Some forms of gnosticism readily accede to human law; none regards any law as having spiritual significance. The element of secrecy and mystery also is a constant. And there is a stubborn persistence in the attempt to prove that some sort of numerology is valid, even though one form failed the founding fathers of the heresy. Blake's statement about how one type of rigidity produces an opposing rigidity is historically true in this case. The effect of the Church's attempts to suppress gnosticism brought about a decided lessening of fluidity in the structure of the Church. The rigid formulation of one Mystery caused the Church to react into a defensive rigidity of another type.

[3] *The Everlasting Gospel* by Blake uses both Christian and gnostic sources, but equally denies the central truths of both. Jesus is not law and love united in the flesh. Yet in earthly life, He was supremely good and supremely capable of accomplishing good. He incarnated all good principles in the flesh. This idea refutes the basis of gnosticism.

this, also, is a dangerous artistic falsification, for what he is saying is not all that simple, however determined he might be to make it sound so. This is the basic problem in his poetics, as obscurantism is Blake's problem. Sugar is sweet. So is the honey in the honeycomb. But to the Psalmist, what was sweeter than the honey in the honeycomb was not the word of love from the Bridegroom, but the Law of the Lord, God's judgments, statutes, commandments. Wesley believed law and love were one, paradoxically related in time, but eternally one. Blake visualized no final judgment to be pronounced by any power outside man. He saw no sweetness in commandment or statute, no love in any discipline imposed from without. At Sinai, what was given to man was not Ten Commandments, but the art of writing in pictures, poetry and art given at once, means of expression given to man's imagination. Of all the authorities accepted by Wesley and rejected by Blake, the most important was the authority of love. Blake thought that for love to assume authority, or for authority to be ascribed to love, would change love into another form of the Elect. Blake's character called Luvah cannot be pictured as other than imperfect, and Luvah was not the hero of Blake's epic.

Wesley's series of *Short Hymns*, though discontinuous, has an action — or, since it is a romance — a Matter.

> My heart is full of Christ, and longs
> Its glorious matter to declare.

His *geste du roi* makes the love manuals seem casual in their analysis of the modes of love, makes *The Faerie Queene* seem uneventful and *Bevis of Hampton* seem brief by comparison. *Short Hymns* has its *longeurs*, but it accumulates all that is sweet and quaint in Wesley's long love affair. His heart dances at the sound of his true love's name. Shouting that name in battle, he laughs at impossibilities. Over his head floats the banner of love. Like a love-sick squire, he reverses one of the Temptations to complain of loss of appetite.

> Thy absence makes my bread a stone.

He plunges to the depths with Jeremiah. In a love story, the very worst thing that can happen is boredom. Only Jeremiah could ever have thought of so gloomy a thing — that God might get bored with us. Wesley could not contemplate the possibility very long. Like Donne, he prayed, "O think mee worth thine anger." And like Donne, he prayed to be made a party to that love affair even despite himself.

> If mercy without end could move
>   So base, so hard a heart as mine,
> Its whole capacity for love
>   Had surely long ago been Thine:
> Lord, for Thine endless mercies' sake
>   My stubborn misery relieve,
> And to Thyself this moment take
>   The heart that I can never give. (ix 157)

"Stubborn misery" might be at times his lot, but he loved One who loved him even in its grip, and in all moods he sang his unfailing surprise at the Cinderella story of the great King of Kings and Lord of Lords who

> fell in love with misery
> And came to claim His bride. (x 349)

He mustered tremendous energy in the exhaustion of repentance. He sang of weariness but never wearied of singing.

His statements of this paradox of law and love use all the heraldic animals of the Bible in a way that reminds one of Blake's dualities, but images a perfect union. The paradox ranges through all areas of ambivalence and draws on the oriental images that portray love relations. Love, being law, is at once dove and serpent, lion and shepherd, leopard and scape-goat, wound and healing, labor and repose, hunger and bread, thirst and wine, He who knocks and an open door. To the thief in the night all things rightfully belong. The unjust judge is justice. The unwearied servant is absolute lord. The treacherous path is eternal home. The sword is peace. The rod is dipped in honey. Fire and fountain are one. The wind that bloweth where it listeth is the sheltering rock. The sun-god whose rays are death from drought is the small rain. The shadow of the Cross is the day-spring. The Sufferer for whom tears shall ever fall is Isaac, whose name is Laughter and dries all tears forever. The Incomprehensible is comprehended within a man's bones and bowels as a woman carries a child in her womb, maturing toward a birth that is death. The singer must in all seasons sing his love, but facing the reality of Love itself, there is difficulty even in saying "I love you," for grammar dissolves its distinctions between pronoun and verb. Act and object become one.

This picture of the lawful Lover is central to all Wesley writings, and its representation was governed by Wesley law. "Jesu, Lover of my soul," said to be the most popular hymn ever written, has gathered around it many legends, one being the legend that it in some way violates this law. It does not.[4] Neither does *Short Hymns* violate Wesley rules for representing anthropomorphic Deity or those special rules governing mysticism. We have proof not only from Charles Wesley but also from the marginalia of that expert, John Wesley, that the book does not actually succumb to mysticism.[5] But so seriously does the author consider once again the mystic ideas, so dangerously does he skirt the rim of that territory, that Bernard Manning says of "Thou Shepherd of Israel" from the section on the Song of Solomon that "nothing short of inspiration keeps the daring emotion sane and reverent and orthodox." [6] This risking much on inspiration is the quality the book shares with *Jerusalem.*

[4] The legend is always based on some assumption that there was one printing only of "Jesu, Lover of My Soul" during the lifetime of the Wesleys and it was sneaked back into the hymnbook after they died. It was printed by them in 1740, in four of their collections, and in the important Madan collection of 1760. Every phrase that has been called objectionable to the Wesleys appears in many other Wesley hymns.

[5] John Wesley, *Works* (3rd ed) VII 294 ff is one of the best statements of Wesley principles. There were important matters of taste, but the imagery that was theologically objectionable was that which suggested the spiritual condition in which self-induced excitation alternated with languor, the languor being excuse for deliberate passivity, and the failure of the opposite state to occur being interpreted as evidence of God's capricious behavior toward man. Either situation was a violation of the concept of law; passivity was violation of the clear law when it caused neglect of the means of grace. The social aspects of Christianity were clear commands and not to be disobeyed; they were commands for which the Wesleys thought they understood some part of the psychological basis to lie in the fact that such contacts work against the isolation intrinsic in the sort of mysticism they considered dangerous. Obedience, however, was not based on any such presumption; the commands to observe the Lord's Supper, and other means of grace, were simply commands. John Wesley's marginalia (IX 43, 97, 217, 379; X 76) and Osborn's comments (IX viii-ix, 406–435) show some criticism; but the notes were private, and it should be recalled that this sort of criticism was done by both brothers; we have no such record of Charles Wesley's criticism of his brother's work. In these few places in this enormous collection, John Wesley saw hints of two things; one, that Christians might not need one another, and two, that God might without provocation withdraw His presence. Love between God and man was in every sense a lawful love, and God could not be pictured as what William Empson in his studies of ambiguity has called "a flirt."

[6] Manning, p 29.

Tell me, O thou whom my soul loveth, where thou feedest, where thou makest thy flock to rest at noon. i.7.

> Thou Shepherd of Israel, and mine,
>   The joy and desire of my heart,
> For closer communion I pine,
>   I long to reside where thou art;
> The pasture I languish to find
>   Where all who their Shepherd obey
> Are fed, on thy bosom reclined,
>   Are screened from the heat of the day.
>
> Ah, show me that happiest place,
>   That place of thy people's abode,
> Where saints in an ecstasy gaze,
>   And hang on a crucified God:
> Thy love for a sinner declare,
>   Thy passion and death on the tree.
> My spirit to Calvary bear,
>   To suffer and triumph with thee.

The subject of Wesley's book is the doctrine of Christian perfection, one so incompatible with Blake's theme that he resumed work on *The Everlasting Gospel* after he finished *Jerusalem* and made it clear that he denied "Christian perfection" even to Christ. He had to think of the Perfect Life as being caught in Time's contraries rather than embodying a perfect paradox, so that the poet might be true to his own interpretation of the Incarnation: God became essentially what man is, so that man might become like God.

The Wesleys believed in the doctrine of Christian perfection, believed that man could live in the world without sin. This beauty of life they could perceive in others. It is characteristic of Charles Wesley that he saw it plainly in his children's nurse. But they could not make it work for themselves, and I am sorry to report that they lived as sinners and died confessing their sins. In *Short Hymns* Charles Wesley looked back over almost half a century of earnest effort to obey the law "Be ye perfect," gave thanks for the guidance of the Spirit and for the human help that had been his favored lot, and surveyed with frank bewilderment his past experience and his present condition. Where were those promised gifts of the Spirit, those fruits of perfection?

Locke said, "Error is the price we pay for progress." Wesley and Blake were committed to progress, but searched for some way to avoid that price. They had difficulty in thus resigning themselves to human error. Blake argued against this resignation of natural religion. Man is infinite, and "less than All cannot satisfy Man." Wesley hoped that the price was not necessary, but he was faced with the existential dilemma: Perfection had commanded him to be perfect, and he was not. The yearning for perfection is universal, and, as both men confess, so are the ancient despairs universal. Blake confesses to them all, and Wesley feels the drag of those old despairs. As his book progresses, he, like Blake, gives imaginative consideration to them. Let us focus on that unit of imagination, the image, and use as example the images of disease.

Wesley's studies in anatomy and materia medica give a sense of emotional reality to the images surpassing even that which may be based on Blake's

---

'Tis there with the lambs of thy flock,
    There only I covet to rest,
To lie at the foot of the Rock,
    Or rise to be hid in thy breast;
'Tis there I would always abide,
    And never a moment depart,
Concealed in the cleft of thy side,
    Eternally held in thy heart. (IX 362–363)

adventures in comparative anatomy with Dr John Hunter. Both poets associate the images with their myth in a manner that differs from the use of Donne (whose imaging of spiritual ills in physical diseases is more in the line of serious wit) or that of W. H. Auden (who uses allegory). Wesley clings to those diseases that had miraculous cure in the Bible; but it is important to note that he feels no actual necessity to do so. For example, he adds a disease that may seem typical of Wesleyan Methodism, a sort of St Vitus Dance (though he does not use that term) of compulsive busyness which may be sin even though the occasions are lawful. One's first reaction is to feel that this is all very cheerful. We know there are miraculous cures for the hand withered by idleness, the fever of fierce desire, the leprosy of a desensitized conscience, the demonic possession of lust, the paralysis of sloth, and that dropsy which has for its symptom an unnatural thirst for praise. We are less sure that there are miraculous cures for Donne's "snatching cramps," his apoplexy of "fast sin," his intermittent piety like a quotidian fever; less sure that miraculous cures are available for the liar's quinsey and the coward's stance that are the subject of Auden's petition. But Wesley has not bought his mythic optimism thus cheaply, and, so intense is his fusing of life and myth, so determined is he not to use his myth as a generality, not to use it as defense against the reality of experience, that one feels through all this certitude a motion toward the despair of determinism. This was the basis of the dissension that for a while had separated the three-fold cord, and had divided him briefly from Whitefield. As Blake acknowledges his own impulse toward determinism in *Jerusalem*, so Wesley makes, not a gesture of understanding toward the other side, but a confession of common sin with them. There are cures, but the onset of disease seems inevitable, evolutionary, in its recurrence.

Faced with the existential dilemma, men state their despair in various vocabularies. Mysticism answers: The Spirit did not move me. Determinism answers: It is God's will, or the doing of Fate. The rationalist answers: Be reasonable and resign yourself to error. Generalization answers: My own memory and history, which is the available sum of memory, prove a general truth: All is not possible. (Blake refutes this by saying the Muses are daughters of inspiration, not memory.) Wesley takes them all into his thinking. Can it be that the gnostics are right, and flesh is totally evil, incapable of good? Can the Calvinists be right, the will of man incapable of choosing heaven, so that man must arrive there by Election not his own? Can it be that, when living experience should be an action that is both personal and mythic, experience will bring only the dead wisdom of generalization? Can the antinomians be right, saying there is no significant distinction between good and evil deeds, virtue and vice?

The Wesleys were highly moral men, devoted to the concept of law and the British Constitution. *Short Hymns* makes a clear distinction between virtue and vice. Yet, in the complexities of human experience, there functions within virtue a more subtle action of contraries. Avarice will move a man to deceive the generosity of others, grasping selfishness will breed avarice in another, carelessness may tempt avarice to sin. But there is an underground rootwork where virtue and vice seem all mixed up. Selfishness may breed habitual generosity in its victims instead of giving birth to further selfishness. Generosity may tempt avarice to an active form of greed such as theft. Zeal for the church may transmute itself into something so like to fraud that the church may become "a den / Of reverend and right reverend thieves." Zeal may beguile a man into the imprudence of giving to the church what should sustain his own family (something the Wesleys had no patience with), and prudence may become over-confident in the means of attaining an end. To exercise only personal charity may be a mask for vanity; but charity may be so organized as to be an easy way out of the more strenuous demands of the giving of oneself with the gift.

The generalizations are my own. Wesley makes the statements, but not in such aphoristic form as brevity forces on me here. He is pondering a story from the Bible both as it is written there, and as he himself had lived it. He goes beyond these observations on the external effects of characteristics to consider more deeply the nature of virtue within itself. Faith is pretext for sloth. Trust in God's providing care by an almost normal process of maturing rots into idleness. Courage becomes cruelty almost, it seems, in the normal course of events. Gentleness curdles into a nauseating lukewarm indifference. Mercy becomes a denial of truth, and stringent insistence on truth erupts in violent denunciation of a brother's faults. *Rigor mortis* alters constancy of spirit into a stiff neck and a stubborn heart. Piety operates as envy of those who were saved "on less severe terms" than oneself. Even the great living reality of a man's conversion experience may be so generalized as to cause him to forget that salvation does not come to all men in ways that are obviously alike. Sins prey upon the energies of youth and upon the feebleness of age, which fears those energies and halters them in enforced introspection. Age congratulates itself upon its sordid virtues once wrath is enfeebled into peevishness and gluttony into finicky appetite.

It is not even this knowledge that distressed Wesley (for the presence of sin came as no surprise to him) so much as his growing distrust of the very value of experience itself. In the depths of his being, he questioned his own assumptions. It seemed that it was the very nature of experience to hurl man from one state to another. And it seemed that all a man learned from it might be these dire generalizations of self-righteousness, so that every achieved virtue served to separate the virtuous man from another segment of sinful humanity, and to that degree to dehumanize him.[7]

The conclusion is nowhere stated in summary form — even that generalization may have seemed dangerous — but it amounts to this: Virtues and vices are different; courage is a virtue and cruelty is a vice. All that exists in time is subject to contrary action. One must submit oneself voluntarily to this contrary action, for "Not to do good is to do ill," and "Sloth is the worst wickedness" (xi 266; x 390). This answer is near to Locke's; true though it be, it is not the final answer. For there is one thing that is simple. All human virtues and even all attributes of God are complex, and must be defined according to some lack, some separation, some deprivation of man. Courage presupposes a threat. Faith is the substance of things hoped for, the evidence of things not seen. Hope implies deprivation. Even faith and hope can tempt a man from "the simplicity that is in Christ." Virtues, like vices, will be "lost in love" (ix 305, 316; xi 249; xiii 18). God's justice exists because it is necessary to divide one thing from another. When man's weakness is no longer the needy corollary to God's needed strength, omnipotence also will be "lost in love" (x 81). Love is not complex, but simple. Love is not an attribute of God, but the law of His nature and His very being, which cannot change. He *is* Love, Jehovah, the great I AM, without need of complement (xi 345, 347).

The conclusion of the matter differs from Blake's conclusion in "mutual forgiveness of all sin." The conclusion has to do with man's relation to God rather than his relation to man. It is not even God's forgiveness that Wesley most desires. Forgiveness was one of the gifts of God, but God Himself was the object of worship. God would give as He saw fit, and there was no bargaining. Wesley hoped for forgiveness, but he said, "I seek not Thine, but Thee," "The Giver, not the gift." It resembles Blake's conclusion at least in one respect: the intense sense of personality of the Divine Humanity.

---

[7] I will submit a report from clear biographical evidence that such was not the result of Wesley "experience." I have said that they determined to submit all dogma to the test of experience, and I have tried to ascertain what dogma stood that testing. All dogma that had to do with man's relation to God held firm. Every change came in the beliefs that make distinction between man and man; every change of heart in the Wesleys brought within the ever-widening circle of their sympathies another sect, another group.

The Wesley hymns had from the first absorbed much of the age in which they were written. The hymns do not refute, but in their own way exemplify the optimism, logic, experimentation of the age. The Wesleys read Pope's "An Essay on Man" in the light of Romans 8:28, and somewhat altered the basis of Pope's optimism.

> Lord, we Thy will obey,
>   And in Thy presence rest.
> We, only we, can say,
>   Whatever is, is best.

They followed Benjamin Franklin's experiments from early stages, and made the creative principle of the Enlightenment into an image of creative love which generates love by its nature and impels movement by its power.

> Touched by the loadstone of Thy love,
>   Let all our hearts agree,
> And ever toward each other move,
>   And ever move toward Thee.

But only in *Short Hymns* did Wesley give any place to deism in his hymns. Among all the ancient forms of despair, he gave it his consideration. It is a loveless religion, but Wesley considered the possibility that it stood in relation to Love, not as a negation, but as a contrary. Was there a great hope in some "universal common sense"? Pope had said that moral law was the basis of man's bliss. Wesley had thought this a shallow layer of optimism covering a deep despair; but if even hope and despair were contraries rather than negations, he would think again.

"Thou Shepherd of Israel'" represents Wesley's nearest approach to mysticism. He took the risk of mysticism's inertia of despair. The hymn is no longer sung (so far as I know). It is too close to the secrecy of the mystic. It has been said the hymn can be understood only "by such as have sat in heavenly places," and hymns are for the public. This hymn is in a danger zone.

In his hymn "The Everlasting Gospel" he drew as near to another danger, near to a religion of moral law. "Thou Shepherd of Israel" is his most fervid hymn; this is his coolest logic, and perhaps can be understood only by men who are so devoted to law that, moved by the logic of the Logos, they will take on the belief of another as lawyers must take on another's position before the law. As logical and legal advocate, Wesley stakes his own position on another man's belief in the conviction that in some way all religions are one. He began to pursue the deist line of reasoning. The message of salvation had inded been "From Adam declared, / To Abraham known," and the patriarchs and prophets were saved by the Word of "anticipated grace" (x 449; xi 434).

The Lamb was slain "from the foundation of the world." Twice the great price had been paid for the nations of the earth. If the first payment was adequate, was the Cross a superfluity — or an abundance of grace? Would the Lamb be cheated in His great bargain? Would the nations at last be His? Was there hope in a universal common sense?

This hymn does indeed lie in a danger zone. So far as I know, it has never been set or sung.[8] I know of no one who could have written it but Charles Wesley, no one else who could have kept it back from deism, and kept it back from that sentimentality (which is the proper offspring of deism) which says, "Think pretty thoughts, and you can fly."

Blake took the same title from the Apocalypse and wrote a poem named *The Everlasting Gospel*. To read a poem through the poet's life, we have been told, may lead to fallacious conclusions about the poem, but it is difficult to forget what we know of Wesley's life and Blake's life, the law-abiding instincts, the rigors of self-imposed discipline, the austerity of mind and chastity of spirit that, accepting all contraries, would yet accept no compromise. The poems in themselves give evidence that Wesley's poem was not written by a loose-thinking sentimentalist nor Blake's by a loose-living libertine. In a special way, the poetry of these enthusiasts is involved in their lives, and in their cases, we read the poems truly only as they stand in relation to ordinary life.

---

[8] But in every nation he that feareth him, and worketh righteousness, is accepted with him. Acts x, 35.

> The everlasting gospel hear
>   To neither time nor place confined,
> Whoe'er thou art, thy Maker fear,
>   The awful author of mankind,
> The great and bountiful and wise,
> Who made, and rules both earth and skies,
>
> The sovereign Cause and End of all,
>   Who justly claims His creature's heart,
> On Him with pious reverence call,
>   From all acknowledged ill depart,
> And, true to thy imperfect light,
> Do what thy heart approves as right.
>
> While thy religious actions show
>   The principle of secret grace,
> Led by a Friend thou dost not know
>   In all the paths of righteousness,
> Heathen, Mahometan, or Jew,
> Thy soul is safe, as God is true.
>
> Surely thou dost even now partake
>   The grace and favour of thy God,
> Accepted for His only sake
>   Who bought the nations with His blood;
> And when He makes thy pardon known,
> Thou know'st that God and Christ are one. (XI 249–250)

They thought something must come into the present social order and save man from the law, something having its source in man (Blake thought) or outside man (Wesley thought), because the law was by nature evil (Blake thought) or by nature righteous (Wesley thought). Once each of them fell afoul the law, and the penalties would have been deaths too dreadful to think about. During their life spans, the number of offenses punishable by death increased from 50 to 350.[9] A ten-year-old child could be hanged for stealing a spoon. A triumph of humanitarianism in 1788 put on the books a weak and ineffective law making it illegal to send a child (some of them four years old) up a *lighted* flue or light a fire to drive him up. Wesley's associates were condemned to transportation for work in the evangelical movement, and few survived that sentence. Field preachers were killed by mobs. The Wesleys had no recourse to law from the vegetables, dogs, and wild bulls that were loosed upon them. The power of the law to protect seemed to diminish as its vindictive nature increased. Blake knew his grounds for complaint against that lawful age. From student days on, Charles Wesley spent hours every week in prisons with condemned men. Whatever the hymns say about the perfect Law, he could hardly have been under the delusion that human law was in a state of perfection. Blake's anarchy is qualified by a myth of the redeemed spirit of Law brooding over fallen Jerusalem. Stated in generalities, the positions seem quite different, but in vision, Blake saw John Wesley as a man raised up by that spirit to meet a crisis in history.

They viewed the city they knew so well with a compassion that makes any other poet of the time seem by comparison almost without social conscience. They did not make the world safe for chimney sweepers nor end human slavery nor remove from the human heart the corruption that comes with power. Not to include Blake in the failure is an insult to his art. It is not as if he did not try. His poems are acts and his pictures are deeds and deserve a place in the failure. The excellent rhetoric book from which I teach tells me helpfully that it is excessively vulgar to close with a pious hope. That is just what I want. Sometimes these two poets can refute our rational grounds for despair; their busy lives can refute quietism, and cause us to wonder if theirs was a final failure; their works can move us at least to a pious hope that those lives and myths may yet have the last word.

9 Helen M. Cam, *Law as It Looks to a Historian* (Cambridge 1956) p 8.

Emily Dickinson and Isaac Watts

IT MUST BE assumed for the purposes of this essay that the Johnson edition of Emily Dickinson's poems is at hand, and the poems may be referred to by number. Time was when it might have been assumed that *Watts Entire* was at hand, not the entire writings of Isaac Watts, but *The Psalms of David Imitated in the Language of the New Testament* and *Hymns and Spiritual Songs*.[1] During the Era of Watts, churches would be satisfied with nothing short of *Watts Entire*. He was the Father of English hymnody. This book, completed in 1719, was the instrument of his Grand Design for the renovation of song in Protestant churches, where, with few exceptions, only metrical versions of the canonical psalms were then sung. Today the book is almost unobtainable, but millions of copies have been sold, and in 1830 when Emily Dickinson was born in Amherst, Massachusetts, a copy was in every pew, schoolroom, and home.

I

Amherst was in the heart of a Watts enclave. When in 1729 Benjamin Franklin brought out the first American edition of Watts's psalms, the book remained unsold in his Philadelphia shop while America continued to sing the Old Version, the New Version, and the Bay Psalm Book. In 1740 George Whitefield swept through the Colonies taking *Watts* with him, and the songs began to be heard in the land. In 1742 Jonathan Edwards sanctioned the use of *Watts* in his church in Northampton. The dates at which other parts of the world adopted Watts's radical ideas will bear witness to Edwards' adventurous and independent spirit, and to his important influence on the history of American hymnody.

Edwards loved music and made a natural association between spontaneous song and religious experience.[2] He admired good congregational singing.

---

[1] *The Poems of Emily Dickinson*, ed Thomas H. Johnson, 3 vols (1955). Poems are numbered chronologically throughout the three volumes. Numbers in parentheses correspond. Watts's psalms retain the numbers of canonical psalms. It is customary to identify his hymns by books (a, b, c) and numbers within the three sections. Texts are quoted from *The Works of Isaac Watts*, 6 vols (1810).

[2] Jonathan Edwards, *Representative Selections*, ed C. H. Faust and Thomas H. Johnson (1935). "Personal Narrative," p 61, "Sarah Pierrepont," p 59, are characteristic statements on music.

His *Faithful Narrative of the Surprizing Work of God in Northampton,* a book introduced in England by Watts, describes how the men of his church could carry "regularly, and well, *three Parts of Musick,* and the *Women* a Part by themselves." [3] The more literal versions of the old metrical psalms were not abandoned in 1742, but as time went on Watts came very near to establishing a new monopoly. In arguments about church music Edwards took Watts's views. He authorized the more controversial free-composed hymns as well as the psalm imitations. In the face of clerical objection, he encouraged the singing outside the church. In Scotland the metrical psalms could be used only in church services; even in choir rehearsals the precentor had to use "practice verses." [4] Judged by their day, Edwards and Watts were *avant-coureurs,* but in the history of Christian song they were reversionary, and represented a turning back to times when church services had been thought of as extensions of home devotions. Northampton, where Edwards preached, Amherst, where Emily Dickinson was born, and South Hadley, where she went to seminary, lie in the Connecticut River Valley in a seven-mile equilateral triangle. For many decades the Valley shared in this tradition fostered by Edwards, a tradition of private and social use of hymns, love of Watts, skillful singing, and amazing liberality in the reception of new music as it appeared.

Each Congregational church has the right to choose its own music. By 1830 *Watts* had been much supplemented with new music, but new music was printed as "Supplementary to Dr Watts," and *Watts Entire* was still the monolithic center of music. It began with "Hush, my dear, lie still and slumber." In the nursery there was "How doth the little busy bee" and " 'Tis the voice of the sluggard." [5] Through school exercises, to college graduation, to social events, to a good selection of funeral hymns, Watts's power extended from the cradle to the grave. Young Austin Dickinson suspected it might go beyond that point, for the Last Judgment seemed to be Watts's special concern, and Emily's brother ascribed to him anything in the general mood of *Dies Irae.*[6]

---

[3] Jonathan Edwards, *A Faithful Narrative of the Surprizing Work of God . . . in Northampton with a large preface by Dr. Watts and Dr. Guyse. London* (1737) 15–16.

[4] Louis Benson, *The English Hymn* (1962) 164. Millar Patrick, *Four Centuries of Scottish Psalmody* (1949) 164–179.

[5] From Watts's *Divine and Moral Songs,* published in 1715.

[6] Millicent Todd Bingham, *Emily Dickinson's Home: Letters of Edward Dickinson and His Family* (1955) 35–36. Two of the hymns that so impressed Austin are by Watts (b, 107, 158), but not "That last great day of doom and woe."

Emily Dickinson
drawing by Hobart V. Hays

By 1850 when Emily returned from seminary and began her career as a poet, Watts was old-fashioned. America was in the tag-end of the Era of Watts. Older members of the congregation by their vote and influence kept him dominant in church services. Young intellectuals were as excited about Emerson as young Mather Byles and his associates had been about Watts in the preceding century.[7]

II

A lyric poet stores in the recesses of being some idea of form that must be satisfied. That idea is affected by rhythms apprehended by the senses, and more deeply affected by rhythms comprehended within the physical frame. As words and as music, the hymns of Watts became involved with Emily Dickinson's vocal cords, fingers, diaphragm, and lungs very early in life.

She wrote at a time when poetry and music were felt to be closely related. She did not know the poetry of her two American contemporaries, Lanier and Whitman, who most successfully exploited elaborate musical forms, opera, cantata, oratorio, chamber music, symphony. "Of Poe," she said, "I know too little to think." [8] She knew the writings of others, notably Long-fellow, who worked from complex musical models, but she had little experience with those forms of music. When she heard Haydn's *Creation* sung in Boston, she merely mentioned "2 concerts" and went on to a detailed description of Mount Auburn Cemetery.[9] When she heard Jenny Lind, she said, "I'd rather have a Yankee." [10] She professed herself content with music made in her own garden, hearing in the natural phenomena the sounds of bugle, banjo, guitar, drums, castanets, bands, trumpet, tambourin, orchestra, ballet, and opera. Amherst was not wanting in the music she loved. Even the whistling in the street delighted her.

She spoke of the singing of Amherst students, the bands that came to town with Welsh's Circus, the Germania Orchestra, Dodsworth's Band; but all her experiments in lyric form were based on music she herself made. At the age of two and a half years she played in some fashion on the first piano she had her hands on.[11] In advanced years she improvised on the rosewood

---

[7] Henry Wilder Foote, *Three Centuries of American Hymnody* (1940) 68, tells of Byles's reaction to Watts, and compares the theology of Watts and Emerson.

[8] *The Letters of Emily Dickinson*, ed Thomas H. Johnson and Theodora Ward, 3 vols (1958) II 649.

[9] Jay Leyda, *The Years and Hours of Emily Dickinson*, 2 vols (1960) I 112, prints a review of the performance. See *Letters* I 36.

[10] *Letters* I 121.

[11] *Letters* I 33.

piano that was the pride of her girlhood. Until her last illness, people came to her home after choir practice to sing for her. She had private music lessons, lessons at Amherst Academy and at Mt Holyoke Seminary. We know her exercise book, the dance tunes, minstrel songs, sentimental ballads she admired. Once she poked fun at her sister's singing of a mournful ditty, but record shows that she herself at sixteen had found the song very touching.[12] She tried in her poems to transmute into high art those characteristic love songs of her era in which death seems to be the ideal of life and love. For a while the songs of Robert Burns held her interest, and she tried out his Scots dialect, stanza forms, and plaintive falling cadences in minor mode (192, 193, 205). She had the poetry and the music she liked. There was no lack of money to buy it and no restriction on her choice.

III

Before considering separate lyrics, I will set down some general statements about the place of Watts among the many influences to be seen in Emily Dickinson's writings. Now that we have her complete, correct texts in chronological order, we are able to read her 1,775 lyrics written over a period of thirty-six years as if they formed a coherent whole. There are esthetic improprieties involved in reading lyric poetry in this way, but there are compensating insights to be gained and carried back with us when we return to a more proper reading of the separate lyrics. One of these insights is a clearer view of her relation to other writers.

The influence of Shakespeare, for example, is perceptible in *Dickinson Entire* in a manner that does not appear in any one lyric. She read the plays, but did not hear them and never saw one staged. The prominent effect was not on the auditory faculty, but rather a stimulus to a special employment of the visual imagination. In the plays, systems of images form almost a separate plot element. In her collected poems, similar systems of images give an effect of drama. The figures do not only grow on themselves (as in all reiterative writing). They enter into the conflicts. They mirror one another, change sides in an argument, combine and re-combine as in multiple valences, entering into combination with conflicting ideas, themes and emotions.

Traces of popular literature float like straws on the surface. Some influences go a little deeper and give rise to gestures, attitudes and situations typical of her day. Her sense of humor was affected by that excellent news-

---

[12] *Letters* I 34, 111.

paper, the *Springfield Republican*, her avowals of literatry taste by the *Atlantic Monthly*. When she speaks as a passionate woman, she uses gestures and situations like those of Mrs Browning and the Brontës, not like *Arcadia* or *The White Devil* or *Moll Flanders*. The influence of the Brontës may go deeper, but that is an unexplored problem. Efforts have been made to give to Emily Dickinson's lost lover a local habitation and a name; it seems to me possible that his habitation was closer to Angria than to Philadelphia.

When she speaks as a child, she takes the stance of most literature of the period. The child is not a genius nor a prodigy; not *Bad Seed* nor *Lord of the Flies*, not inherently evil, but innately good; naive and knowing, obtuse and intuitively wise, meek and yet enabled to rebuke his elders by moral superiority and spiritual qualities. Her child characters take on an air of martyrdom from Little Jo and Little Eva, but bear no such flaming social messages. They may sound like the tots in Peter Parley, but she did not maintain that coy posture for long. They momentarily suggest Elsie Dinsmore, but Emily Dickinson was too good-natured to assume the habits of revenge necessary to write a genuine *Elsie*. George F. Whicher closed his interpretive biography by comparing her to Huck Finn. We mark also her kinship to Alice, although she read Huck and Alice late in life, if indeed she ever read them.[13] Their spirits are present not as mediumistic controls, but as part of the *Zeitgeist*.

As the work of reconstructing her world progresses, it becomes increasingly clear that her poems are deep-rooted in Amherst soil. The sum total of influences and explication of details may never budge us from the conviction that she was one of the least influenced of poets, when you get to the heart of the matter. We may feel that we need no knowledge of a poet's world for the larger purposes of literature; but we need knowledge of her grammar if only to prevent an occasional misreading, as we need knowledge of Chaucer's petrified dative and Shakespeare's neuter possessive pronoun. We need knowledge of systems of thought and speech if only to discount them as irrelevant to the poet's originality. These examples from familiar literature are not given for the purpose of emphasizing their importance, so much as to offer them as a species of disclaimer, a model for assessing various influences from the less familiar hymn literature. Influences may be present, and may be often present, and yet have no great importance. Their significance must be variously qualified and assessed.

---

13 It is not certain that Emily Dickinson read the stories of Huck Finn and Alice. Austin's daughter owned an 1872 edition of Alice. T. W. Higginson read the stories, and often shared his enthusiasms with Emily Dickinson.

The formal influence in all her poetry is the hymn. When music is considered along with hymn texts, that influence is seen as pervasive. Her poetry was written as Watts's was written, as most hymns are written, *par-odia*, to an existing tune.

If a hymn be defined as a lyric intended for congregational singing, she wrote none. Her poems were not so intended, have never been so used, would not be appropriate to such use. Yet she wrote no epic, drama, fiction, essay, sonnet, or villanelle, but only something she called hymns or psalms. Hymn meters set her meters. The range of the reading voice is restricted to hymn range. Vocabulary is impregnated with hymn vocabulary and strictly circumscribed by New England gentility. Questions are posed and answered with reference to religious thought.

She wrote nineteenth-century hymns. They differ from eighteenth-century hymns (especially from those by Watts) by their greater metrical freedom, freer use of enjambment, use of more images with no scriptural source. The voice is that of a lone singer rather than the voice of the congregation assembled. Lay writers knew and cared little about dogma and systematic theology. The songs at their worst were modes of sentimental self-expression, not songs in praise of God. Dozens of noble exceptions rush to mind from nineteenth-century hymnody, the more readily because the noble exceptions remain in use — but the generalizations hold.

As she adopted at times the stance of Dickens without ever adopting his social conscience, so in like manner she adopted gestures and situations from nineteenth-century hymns. Many of the hymns have an aura of medieval Catholicism like that which surrounds some work of Scott, Keats, Coleridge. She also could set up a typical situation of a medieval mystic. "Oh, Shadow on the Grass" (1187) is a beautiful incantation suggesting the medieval song "I sing of a maiden." But the point to that poem is the same as the point to her other poems that hint of a mystic encounter: there was no encounter, no certainty that the shadow was anything other than a shadow.

If I were able to perceive any evidence of the peculiar regional "transcentalism" and "Unitarianism" that have been thrust upon her by some critics, I should be glad to point them out. There are only such elements of mysticism and transcendentalism as are common to all orthodox Hebrew and Christian thinking. She was no Unitarian. The separate phrases of the Apostles' Creed make a fairly comprehensive index of her religious preoccupations.

She was a Puritan with a Puritan's attitude toward the Establishment, which is by definition a desire to purify it and recall it to the right ways. In

her life, Watts had preempted control of the Establishment, and she saw a
great deal that seemed wrong with Watts.

From first to last in all her writings, she never consciously alluded to him
in any tone but criticism, any spirit but one of refutation. Her refusal to be
awed by hell was more systematic than Huck's parody of the Sunday School
lesson. Her statements on instructing children in uglification and derision
are more impassioned than Alice's parodies of Watts's moralizing. It was
1862 when Alice's more sympathetic logician took her boating and silenced
Watts's Busy Bee and laid out his Sluggard for his final repose. Emily Dickinson had been trying since 1850 to perform these last rites. Pending the day
when computer experts shall program the texts of Watts, Dickinson and the
King James Version, and prove by IBM that she attacked Watts's version,[13a]
we must take her word for it. Her celebrated statement on the subject (1545)
says nothing is wrong with the Bible. It is the manner of singing it that is
wrong. This poem is the record of her most careful revision. She tried out
thirteen adjectives before she made a choice: "Had but the Tale a warbling
Teller," children would listen gladly. Knowing Watts, one can see the consistency in her contradictory moods. Her marriage of jest and passion does
not seem an unequal yoking of believer and unbeliever, but a true oneness
of substance. Through every avenue of life, she learned from the Father of
English hymnody how she would never write. That is an important thing
for an author to learn. In her writing, she did not depart from the genre he
fathered.

Mr Austin Warren says that in some poems she "creates a counterpoint or
descant on Watts." [14] These musical forms must arrive at harmony with the
cantus firmus. She does perform this sort of musical exercise, but beside Mr
Warren's musical analogies, I will place another.

Miss Phyllis Bartlett called Emily Dickinson "an unorthodox religious
poet — like Hopkins." [15] Unorthodox not in theology (Father Hopkins was
orthodox) but in the poetic process that was Miss Bartlett's special study.
Orthodoxy of poetics must be defined with reference to time and place.
Hopkins and Emily Dickinson began with simple metrical ideas, he with
the rhythms of common speech, choruses, refrains, nursery rhymes, weather

---

[13a] Bible concordances have long existed; *A Concordance to the Poems of Emily Dickinson*,
edited by S. P. Rosenbaum, has just been published by Cornell; *Watts Entire* may wait some
time.

[14] Austin Warren, p 105 in *Emily Dickinson: A Collection of Critical Essays*, ed R. B. Sewall
(1963): see also John Crowe Ransom, p 99–100. See Thomas H. Johnson, *Emily Dickinson: An
Interpretive Biography* (1960) 70–77.

[15] Phyllis Bartlett, *Poems in Process* (1951) 84–87.

saws,[16] she with hymn meters. Both poets developed metrical tactics that were unorthodox for their time and place. Now, descant and counterpoint describe methods of handling a hymn that were orthodox in the Valley. An unorthodox method was also at work in her poetry.

The method is parody in the usual sense: the imitation of an art form that handles any element of art so as to criticize the original form with more or less serious intent. In our day, Mr T. S. Eliot's influence has converted the method to orthodoxy by his use of parody to produce poetry of serious intent. He frustrates the expectations raised by some familiar verse form, and turns the reader from lyric mood to critical evaluation of statements commonly associated with the original form. Emily Dickinson handled various elements of words and music so as to comment on statements commonly associated with the hymn form. Watts's is a statement of unwavering faith. She said that "we believe and disbelieve a hundred times an Hour, which keeps believing nimble."[17] In her determination to "Tell all the Truth but tell it slant" (1129), she used her most un-dear preceptor as a monolith from which to slant, referring to his uprightness to define her angle of variation, whatever it might be at the moment.

IV

She started with simple methods, parodying hymns and prayers as she sat in church and in letters, writing sermon parodies for *Forest Leaves*, the school paper. Her brother joined the game. He sent her a "psalm" to be sung to Greenville, a hymn tune composed by Jean Jacques Rousseau, and her answering letter was "Variations on Greenville."[18] It would be a *coup* to be able to attribute to Austin the parody on Greenville, "Go tell Aunt Dinah the old gray goose is dead," but these youthful efforts do not survive. Such pranks did not contravene piety or decorum. Her sermons were considered innocuous. Austin Dickinson knew that his letters were read by the whole family.

The whole family interjected into common discourse the rhythmic phrases of Bible and hymn, quoted or in parodic form. Mr Dickinson wrote to tell his son that work had begun on the Amherst & Belchertown Railway, and the family would here "set up our Ebenezer." He alluded to I Samuel 7:12, a hymn by Robinson, and the doctrine of the Covenant, but he added an

---

[16] Gerard Manley Hopkins, "Author's Preface," *Poems*, 3rd ed (1948) 9.

[17] *Letters* III 728.

[18] *Letters* I 201, 234–236. George Frisbie Whicher, *This Was a Poet* (1938) 176.

exultant and capitalized HA! HA!! [19] Emily planned to go to heaven via
that railway, as certain of her destination "As if the checks were given," that
is, as if the conductor had already taken up her ticket (1052). The relation
of this poem to Watts has been recognized.[20] It is more a counterpoint on
Watts than a parody. A Valentine she wrote was published in the Amherst
College paper in 1850; it contains a parody of Watts's Psalm 72.[21] Her first
published poem (3) was a Valentine printed that year in the *Springfield
Republican*. The verse rhymes some of the cliches in Latin and English that
were offered to the young as guides for conduct, among them two lines from
Watts. Many later poems used the two lines. With increasing complexity
they were made to deal with important themes.

The first is "How doth the busy bee." In two very early poems that ante-
date the Valentine there are bees, buzzing and courting flowers. From the
Valentine of 1850 on, her bee was a defiant counter-emblem to Watts's
emblem, and her sententiae dispute his. Bees are idle. One poem (994)
speaks of an abstemious bee, but one is forced to the conclusion that she
was being ironic about the bee's exercise of self-control. For bees at best are
irresponsible creatures (138, 1343), indiscriminate in their pursuit of *la
dolce vita* (1627), and unmindful of the Judgment Day (620). They are
seducers, traitors, buccaneers, given over to apostacy and heresies (81, 128,
134, 206, 213, 214, 230, 661, 896, 1220, 1224, 1339, 1526, 1628). Watts's bee
also was "a reckless Guide." [22] Rascals though they were, they wore the very
gems of heaven (916) and, with regard to the dichotomy of ordained versus
contingent grace, they lived in this life by "Fuzz ordained, not Fuzz contingent" (1405). The admirable verse epistle from his friend Fly to Bee
(1035) may parody Watts's less inspired hymns, some of which sound as if
they might conclude "Yours truly, I. Watts" — but perhaps not.

When her nephew started to school, she sent him a poem with instructions
that it be given to his teacher (1522). The bee's religion is not "Industry and
Morals," but "the divine Perdition / Of Idleness." She footnoted the poem
with two quotations from Revelation, one (Rev. 21:8) cited to "Jonathan
Edwards," though she might have better cited it to Watts, who rhymed it
and put it close beside his Bee:

---

[19] Leyda I 233.

[20] James Davidson, "Emily Dickinson and Isaac Watts," *Boston Public Library Quarterly* VI
(1954) 141–149.

[21] *Letters* I 92.

[22] *Letters* II 604.

> ev'ry liar
> Shall have his portion in the lake
> That burns with brimstone and with fire. (Song 15)

The other (Rev. 22:7) she signed "Jesus": "And let him that is athirst come." She thought boys had a hard life. She did not want Gilbert subverted by Wattsian notions, and for all her jokes, she dealt with vital matters.

The other line in the Valentine is taken from "There is a land of pure delight."

> Could we but climb where Moses stood,
>   And view the landscape o'er,
> Not Jordan's stream nor death's cold flood
>   Should fright us from the shore.   (b, 66)

Moses' distant glimpse of the Promised Land from Mt Nebo she associates with "the Hill of Science," from which eminence the poet views with sarcastic rapture the "transcendental prospect" spread by the learned before her eyes.

Like the Bee, this line meanders through her poetry. It becomes (112) the "Voice of the Sluggard Emily," who longed to sleep "Thro' Centuries of Noon," but was prevented by various personifications of industry.

Then (168) she began to turn Watts's leading character against Watts as she did with the Bee. Moses himself opposes the narrowminded "Savants" who categorize nature. In this poem there is a hint of the same theme on which the Bee was made to comment: justice. Moses was allowed to view the Promised Land only from afar. Was the edict that kept him from Canaan a just one? Watts did not question its justice, but who can trust a Savant? The hint in this poem becomes the theme of the next one.

> Old Man on Nebo! Late as this —
> My justice bleeds — for Thee!   (597)

Then, as she had accumulated the Sluggard into her poems about the Bee, she began to pick up others of Watts's *Divine and Moral Songs*. Song 15, quoted above, tells of the fate of Ananias, "struck dead / Catch'd with a lie upon his tongue." Another *Moral Song*, "Innocent Play," is a bland injunction against wading, an argument from analogy that Emily Dickinson found irrelevant, illogical, and annoying: "If we had been ducks, we might dabble in mud." She fretted a good deal about the justice of that edict. One poem (1201) lumps the fates of Moses, Ananias, and the young dabbler as three prime examples of miscarriage of justice.

In similar manner more serious questionings of divine justice accumulate arguments from other encounters of Moses with Jehovah (Ex. 3:2; 33:11–23; Num. 11; 14:14; Deut. 3:27; 5:4–5; 31:1). Some experience of her own is made analogous to the incidents. As the bush had burned without being consumed, as the prayer on Sinai for full sight of God's glory had been denied, as the view of Canaan had been brief, so had she burned with cold fire, had been denied, had lost some earthly paradise after one glimpse (576, 597, 694, 1247, 1733).

The progressions of *Watts Entire* do not falter: The justice of God and the mercy of God are one attribute of Holiness which cannot be in conflict with Itself, which controls and contains all that exists. She took up her themes in youthful exuberance, with some ironic qualifications even then, but on the whole confident that the ideas could be domesticated into common parlance. There came comic rebellions, passionate rebellions, moods when the brief vision seemed worth anything it cost, moods when she felt that love and poetry had been born "coeval" from the glimpse, moods when she suspected poetry came more from the deprivation than the vision. She and Watts agreed that the matter was worth thinking about all one's life, and agreed that for whatever went wrong or came out right God was responsible. That is a fairly large area of agreement, but it left room for the exercise of the critical implement of parody. Watts seemed to disregard experience. He moved all too inevitably by progressions that were all too simple to his four-fold chord where mercy and righteousness, truth and peace met and kissed.

V

Art, Calvin said, is characterized by sobriety, simplicity, measure.[23] Emily Dickinson preferred her drunken bee, her shimmering multiplicity of statement, an ideal of song as free, improvisatory, with "Keyless Rhyme" (503) and "phraseless Melody" (321).

Watts added to Calvin the tenets of neoclassicism: confidence in the validity of generalization, the congruence of faith and science, the reasonableness of the Christian dogma. A disciple and promulgator of Newton's theories, he took a sweeping cosmic view to which panorama the Cross stood center and cynosure. Emily Dickinson's world was fragmented, her insistence on her own smallness was almost obsessive. His serene didacticism

---

[23] Leon G. Wencelius, *The Word of God and the Reformed Faith* (1943) 156–181. A. Mitchell Hunter, *The Teachings of Calvin* (1950) 272–294. Henry R. Van Til, *The Calvinist Concept of Culture* (1959) 107–114.

contrasts with her plea to be taught, her inability to learn, her refusal to communicate. He thought clarity of statement was possible, and was a duty. She said, "All men say 'What' to me." [24] Irrefutable logic was his organizing principle; hers was her own sensibility, from which her mind was never removed. Timeless verities were his theme; hers was the supreme importance of the fluctuating moment. Firmly phrased abstract truth plunged her into dread of losing reality in abstraction. He was public, ceremonious; she valued privacy to the point of perverseness.

Critics sometimes place undue emphasis on the unusual housing arrangements recounted in The Lives of the Poets. These two unusual cases were both important because the housing arrangements made possible the very writing of the poetry, and because they are archetypes of the poetry. It is unusual for a maiden lady to remain in her own home, seeing only those whom she chose to see. It is unusual for a gentleman to go for a week's visit to the home of the Lord Mayor of London and stay the rest of his life, thirty-four years a welcome and honored guest. One poet had no public life, one no private life, and the temperaments that chose to live thus mark the poetry.

Calvin approved of congregational song. Neoclassical poetry found a fit subject in the public aspects of man's life. But Watts, beyond the bounds of either esthetic and in defiance of both, chose as his special task the formulation of private emotions into public, choric song. Emily Dickinson came more and more to be offended by what seemed to her a grossness of public statement. Even a letter addressed jointly to herself and her sister drew a rebuke to the sender; letters were private matters. She shunned men and women (women especially) because "they talk of Hallowed Things, aloud — and embarrass my Dog." She had a growing "appetite for silence." [25] She found she "could not bear to live — aloud" (486).

No other writer of church song has accepted such a burden of restrictions as Watts bore. Rebellion against one restriction made him the Father of English Hymnody. Acceptance of the others made him the unsurpassed writer of classic hymns. Writing for all congregations, some with no official litany, he made the songs a litany, a careful and complete pronouncement of classic Christian doctrine in its fulness, covering all occasions. The doctrine had to be clear to the lowest mind; the poetry must give no offense to his own cultured congregation. Preserving Augustan purity of diction, he abjured Augustan ornamentation, excluding any metaphor that might mislead those unaccustomed to the oblique statements of art. Mnemonic devices, usually of an undignified nature, must be used if they could be made con-

[24] *Letters* II 415.   [25] *Letters* II 415; III 927.

sonant with dignity so that his verses would cling to the memory of the illiterate. Abandoning his pride in intricate Greek and Latin prosody, he worked patiently within the narrow repertory of the tunes these people knew and would sing.

The one restriction he violated was, of course, the use of the Bible. Metrical psalms strove for literal accuracy, a one-to-one relation to Holy Writ. Watts established a new relation between church song and scripture. Each hymn, complete in itself, must send the reader back to the Bible; must exist as a work of art, yet form a gloss subsuming within brief compass the existing glosses and commentaries. His success can still dazzle experts. He knew the work of the lower criticism (which seeks to establish correct Biblical text) and the higher criticism (which on the basis of corrected text makes historical, literary, and doctrinal judgments), and — to summarize his position — every song is essentially an act of criticism, of interpretation. All attacks on his work arose from his refusal to accept Scripture without altering it, from his determination to interpret its relevance to present experience.

He worked alone. No pope, bishop, college or committee asked him to undertake his task. *Watts Entire* is a shocking example of Protestant individualism. It did not seem to Emily Dickinson sufficiently individualistic, yet when I read any attempt to declare her theological position, whether by critics who deplore her mischievous ways or by those who exult in her audacity, I hear again the praise and blame given to Watts from the first publication of his hymns until now: "Spontaneity threatens tradition. To criticize that which should be received in literal form is dangerous. Human experience should be interpreted by doctrine, not doctrine by experience." The objections are perennial, for Puritan pride will speak, however softly, its demonic *Non serviam* in every age, not to God, but to the earthly fathers of its spirit, Watts to Calvin and Cranmer, Emily Dickinson to Watts and Edwards.

V I

The three hymnbooks used by Emily Dickinson during the years when she went to church are the chief source of information about her knowledge of church song.[26] Daily from earliest years she knew the words, music, and

---

[26] *The Psalms, Hymns, and Spiritual Songs of the Rev. Isaac Watts, D.D., to which are added, Select Hymns, from other Authors; and Directions for Musical Expression,* ed Samuel Worcester. Known as *Watts & Select,* it was first published in 1819.

Church Psalmody . . . Selected from Dr. Watts and Other Authors, ed Lowell Mason and David Greene (1831). *Village Hymns . . . a Supplement to Dr. Watts's Psalms and Hymns,* ed Asahel Nettleton (1824). Used also at Mt. Holyoke Seminary.

styles of singing. Watts predominates; but all periods of church song are represented, the old metrical psalms, the era of Watts and his disciples, the era dominated by the Wesleys, the early romantic writers. Family letters and records, including the valuable background material compiled by Mr Jay Leyda, give some idea as to which songs were especially important. Additional information is found in books, periodicals, and music known to have been in the home. All this material should be read against the history of American hymnody, with special attention to the disputes that have always gone along with church song.

In quotation or in parody, I find allusions to the hymns of Burkitt, Watts, Doddridge, Stennett, John Burton, Newton, Cowper, Robinson, and possibly Kelly, Hart, and Simon Browne. Later writers who are prominent in family records are Mrs Barbauld, H. K. White, Bishop Heber, and James Montgomery.

The egregious omission is the Wesley hymns. About thirty of the hymns are in the three hymnbooks, most of them anonymous. Jonathan Edwards' suspicion of the very word *Arminian* may have been still active in the Valley to exclude them. If so, some apt hymnologists did the excluding. The three meters that interest me most with reference to Dickinson poetry are attributed to sound Calvinist names. "Jesu, Lover of my soul" is ascribed to Cowper, "Blow ye the trumpet" to Toplady, and "Love divine" to Whitefield. Wesley hymns may have been sung, but there is no mention of them. No single phrase indicates that the Dickinsons ever sang one — and Wesley phrases adhere powerfully to the memory.

In a study of prosody, however, the absence of the Wesleys' hymns does not by any means exclude Wesley influence. Watts wrote almost altogether in three stanza forms. Charles Wesley used almost a hundred. Subsequent writers adopted Wesley meters, and long before 1850 the influence had pervaded hymnody.

Metrical influences of the English romantic poets also are present. It is, as a matter of fact, chancy business proving any specific metrical influence in the lyrics of any American poet of this period if the poet went to church. The English romantic poets, Shelley excepted, had their lyrics conscripted into the service. Sir Walter Scott's version of *Dies Irae* from *The Lay of the Last Minstrel* is in two of her three early hymnbooks, properly ascribed to him. But the meters of other poets are present when their actual words are not. For example, Byron's *Hebrew Melodies* were used in other hymnbooks, but not in these three. In two of the books, however, is the song "Daughter of Zion, awake from thy sadness," not Byron's, but using Byron's general mood and his dactyllic tetrameter.

She quit going to church, but she read hymns and practiced hymn tactics all her life. She knew the hymns of Whittier first from magazine publication, then later in book form. She mentioned the work of F. W. Faber. The light verse movements of Ray Palmer of the American romantic school seem to have made themselves felt in two poems at least (34,1237).

In English hymnody, the next great era was brought in by the writers of the Oxford Movement. Emily Dickinson did not speak of these writers, except once to tell her sister-in-law how to spell *Puseyite*, but her sister Lavina owned an 1847 edition of *The Christian Year* by Keble, which is the fountainhead of that hymnody. Keble often rhymed long with short lines, a thing seldom done in eighteenth-century hymns. Emerson also used the trick, and she knew Emerson well; but her experimenting in this mannerism appears in association with phrases that make it appear that she imitated Keble. H. F. Lyte's broken pentameters — as opposed to the solider pentameters of Old 50th and Walworth — seem to have served her as model (381,382). One poem (964) by mood, content, stanza form, and use of dialogue, suggests an experiment based on J. M. Neale's hymn from the Greek, "Art thou weary?"

American hymnody reacted to the revival of Unitarian interest in church song, and names that were dear to her were signed to hymns that contributed to that revival: Thomas W. Higginson, J. G. Holland, Emerson, Hale, Lowell, Pierpont, Bryant, Longfellow, Parker. Names of other writers she admired are in hymnbooks in her home. "The night is come, like to the day" is from *Religio Medici*. Five hymns by Mrs Browning are in Henry Ward Beecher's *Plymouth Collection* (1850). I know of no use of the Brontë hymns in American hymnbooks before the 1870s, but the poems were known to her in her girlhood and the influence is apparent. She spoke of no other public event with such delight as she felt in the visits of Edwards A. Park; few names are more honored in American hymnography.[27] But the important name is Watts.

Watts's early book *Horae Lyricae* shows him a resourceful and ambitious metrist. He set insoluble problems for himself and did not solve them completely; no poem is satisfactory throughout as poetry, though there are bril-

---

[27] *Letters* I 271–272. Park's *Sabbath Hymn Book* was the most scholarly of the century; five copies from the Dickinson home are in Houghton Library. When Louis Benson wrote *The English Hymn*, his only important predecessor in the study of hymnology was *Hymns and Choirs* (1860) by Park and Phelps.

liant spots. But he learned skill in the weighing and disposition of syllables, and *Watts Entire* is a metrical triumph. The texture of his verse differs as widely from that of his predecessors in church song as does that of Emily Dickinson from, say, Mrs Barbauld's, whom she admired. She and Watts were well matched as metrists, with delicate ears for nuance, sensitive awareness of musical conventions absorbed from childhood on, and audacity to revolutionize a metrical situation.

In all hymnody they are the two notorious offenders with false rhyme. They loved it. Watts's rhyme is not "slip-shod," but works by phonetic laws that are easily seen when his rhyme-words are examined. Emily Dickinson, beginning her career with a large vocabulary of rhyme-words learned by ear from hymns, including a large vocabulary of false rhyme learned from Watts, went as far beyond his liberties as he went beyond the conventions of English verse.[28] About 50% of his rhyme is false. He felt, however, a need for true rhyme at the close of a hymn. His half-rhymed stanzas often change to full rhyme in the last stanza, and about 77% of his final rhyme is true, even when one counts as false those rhymes allowed by convention (come-home, abroad-God, word-Lord, etc). Years of usage had accustomed her to expect a hymn to close in true rhyme on a simple major chord (called in her hymnbooks "the flat key") or minor chord ("the sharp key"). The ear, anticipating the norm, will be lulled only by the expected sound. Where she departed from that convention, her sound patterns should be considered in assessing her poetic intention, for it is at this point the hymn convention is most vulnerable.

VII

Church singing in 1700 was an example of the comic as defined by Henri Bergson, in its adherence to half-forgotten traditions declared sacrosanct and ossified by the accretion of ignorance on ignorance. Only historical myopeia can foist the blame on Calvin. Calvin took the best available help and pro-

---

[28] Watts divided the phonetic spectrum in two parts, apparently, and freely rhymed any dark vowel sound with any other, any light vowel sound with any other. He did not rhyme dark with light vowels, either in vowel rhyme or suspended rhyme, except in a few cases. One is the sibilant; any sibilant seemed to serve in itself as a rhyme without consideration of the preceding vowel sound; thus, he occasionally rhymed peace-pronounce, etc. The long *o* rhymed thus: boast-frost-trust; hope-prop-up; shone-son; stroke-flock; goat-foot, road-clod; groan-dawn. But long or short *o* did not rhyme with *a, e, i*. In vowel rhyme such matchings occur more frequently than in suspended rhyme, but the rule is the same. Any nasal consonant was made equal to any other. He rhymed *m* with *n*, *n* with *nd* and *ng*, and (rarely) *m* with *ng*. F and *v* are equivalent. Both he and Emily Dickinson sounded *l* and *r* so lightly that the sounds might be ignored in rhyming. He rhymed thought-not-note-vault-court. Emily Dickinson rhymed dark with light vowel sounds, and accepted many consonants as equivalent that were distinguished by Watts. Whicher (244–246) lists some of her principles of rhyming.

duced a psalter coherent in esthetic principle, rich in metrical variety, grave
and impressive in its beauty beyond any authorized metrical psalter in English. It was not that England from 1549 to 1700 had no better poets and no
better scholars than Sternhold and Hopkins. By 1600 English cathedral
music was acknowledged to hold the supreme position among the nations of
Europe. Editorial policy reduced Scotland to common measure, England
almost to common, short and long measure alone, and did it during the great
days of English song.

There is nothing wrong with CM, SM, LM.[29] They are fine lyric forms,
capable of carrying great weight, capable also of moving lightly and swiftly,
instinct with energy in the hands of a good metrist. Watts used them almost
entirely, and Emily Dickinson worked some of her best magic with them.[30]
But in 1700 (when Huguenot singing was noted for its excellence) the
psalms were lined out. A leader read a line (two lines if the stanza be considered as a quatrain), then the congregation sang it. Thus stanza forms
that should have given Watts units of 32, 28 and 26 syllables actually had
only half that length as units of grammar and sense. Watts eventually did
discredit the wretched practice, but in the meantime had to end-stop every
couplet lest grammar be disrupted.

Tunes that Queen Elizabeth had called "Geneva Jigges" were sung in
1700 at tempi that dragged the songs out of shape and intelligibility. All
tunes were strictly syllabic, one note to each syllable of text. Originally the
tunes had no musical bars and moved freely, but bars were added in the
interest of "correctness." By 1700 the only notation was minim and semibreve, and notes had only two possible time relations, one to one or one to
two. It suited the convenience of printers to set the notes on the staff, not

[29] Common measure is ballad stanza, the syllabic arrangement being 8.6.8.6, rhyming ABAB,
or half-rhymed ABCB. Written as a couplet, it is the fourteener. Short measure drops two syllables from the first line (6.6.8.6). Written in two lines, it is "Poulters measure, which giueth xii
for one dozen and xiij for another," nicknamed by George Gascoigne in *The Steele Glas* (1576).
Poulters, like bakers, could be fined for giving short measure, and added a precautionary item
or so to their dozens. Long measure is the English equivalent of the Latin stanza used by St
Ambrose in early stanzaic Christian song. It has eight syllables to the line (8.8.8.8), rhymes consecutively (AABB) or is cross-rhymed (ABAB). One of Watts's psalms in LM is half-rhymed, but
the practice was almost unknown. All psalm measure is iambic, but tunes could accommodate
an opening trochaic, spondaic, or pyrrhic foot. Except two lines in Old 50th, all rhyme is
masculine.

[30] Five variant stanza forms are in the Old Version, Psalm 50, 112, 113, 122, 148. Watts used
these, but wrote at least one version of every psalm in the three basic forms. His hymns used
only the stanza of Old 148th. In *Watts Entire* only 23 of 697 lyrics are in variant meters, plus
five doxologies in Old 148th. Both he and Emily Dickinson used CM most frequently. The two
stanza forms she used most frequently after CM are Sevens and Sixes, and a form called Common Particular Meter (8.8.6.8.8.6), neither of which was used by Watts.

above or below it, and some tunes were removed from normal singing range. Leaders unfortunately knew enough music to read a semibreve on A, but knew little more, and had no saving historical knowledge of the questionable sources of all these disparate correctnesses. Results proved how dangerous a thing a little learning can be.

Emily Dickinson saw the opposite extreme. Remembering that Wesley hymns were written for use outside the sanctuary, one can say there never has been a time when an English-speaking church was so open to all influences, sacred and secular. Watts's words might be associated with almost any style of music.

Until 1838 music in her church was unaccompanied (as Calvin had advised) but not (as he also had advised) performed in unison. Like the singing described by Jonathan Edwards, it was harmonic. In 1838 her church bought a bass viol, and in 1850 installed an organ, a rare luxury. In 1838 the church adopted a hymnbook edited by Lowell Mason. Under the sponsorship of the Handel and Haydn Society of Boston, Mason was editing, composing, lecturing, establishing schools of church music, keeping in touch with European music. Henry Ward Beecher, a friend of the Dickinsons', and his organist John Zundel were launching many changes along the lines laid down by Mason. The entire Dickinson family attended the singing schools at the church.

The old syllabic tunes were in use, and are today. Dundee, one of twelve common measure tunes which in Scotland formed an unexpandable canon of sacred music, was then and is now much loved. This common measure is Emily Dickinson's basic tune. "Because I could not stop for Death" (712) is correct psalm form, perfectly syllabic, each note a minim or semibreve. It is a parody only in the sense that the poem cringes away from the sobriety, simplicity, and measure of a funeral hymn, protesting against the civility with which the civilized must accept death. That obliging gentleman who stops for her is no wooer. He is the village undertaker, suave and macabre.

Tunes that flexed psalm measure from strict syllabic form began to appear the year after the first publication of Watts's hymns, and by 1850 the variations were almost infinite. Such a stanza as "How many times these low feet staggered" (187) would sing, for example, to Greenville, each line beginning with a trochee, and with an added syllable in each of the lines of the last stanza. The poem is symmetrical as a musical arrangement. "There's a certain slant of light" (258) is symmetrical when groupings of short notes are observed. To a greater degree than is apparent from reading words alone, the stanza form of a hymn varies within a song. In the singing of hymns, stanzas are not reiterated in monostrophe; the meaning of words and the weight of syllables will enforce a certain amount of variation and syncopation, and the amount varies, increasing as the poetry is accepted as expressive, rather than imitative art. When Emily Dickinson went to school, there was about half a century behind her during which poetry had been taught from rhetoric books which emphasized musical analogies. The margins of her hymnbooks give standard markings to indicate expression in musical terms, and the marks relate to words, for no music is printed in the books. The relation of these marks to the markings in her manuscripts has never been investigated, but it is agreed that her markings indicate some sort of directions for expression, in addition to or instead of grammatical punctuation.[31] Although she carried her experimenting beyond the bounds that were allowed, most of her poems could be accommodated by practices of her extremely liberal era. Tunes known to her could give the musical effects she is asking for by her frequent use of a divided line, and her occasional use of internal rhyme. A change from common to short measure (625) could be accommodated, even when one line ("No Lifetime — on Them") was shortened to five syllables, as it appears in the one-volume edition.

Under the influence of Mason, choirs used through-composed music such as Schubert wrote for *Die schöne Müllerin*. Opening and closing in strophic form, the songs had sections between which ignored strophic form. Emily Dickinson would set the third of four stanzas in *durchkomponiert* style (527), or merge the second and third of four stanzas (553) so that a rather commonplace song rises to its climax in lovely romantic words and tune: "Gethsemane — Is but a Province — in the Being's Centre." In "After great pain" (341) a more elaborate musical idea is at work. It opens and closes in pentameter. The middle section gives the effect of long measure set in *durchkomponiert* manner. The Ambrosian stanza exists here only to be violated, but it does exist. One feels, consciously or unconsciously, how easy it would have been to write the lines in LM, thus:

> The feet, mechanical, go round
> A way of Ought, or Air, or Ground,
> A wooden way, regardless grown,
> A quartz contentment like a stone.

[31] See my *Garrick's Jubilee* (1964) 200–212 for discussion of the work of Joshua Steele, from which came the influence on scansion in rhetoric books. Edith Perry Stamm, "Emily Dickinson: Poetry and Punctuation," *Saturday Review* (March 30 1963), associates the markings with the system in Noah Porter's *Rhetorical Grammar*, a book which makes use of Steele's system. For other comment on Emily Dickinson's markings, see Austin Warren as previously cited. Also in Sewell's collection of critical essays, see R. P. Blackmuir, "Emily Dickinson's Notation," 78–85. See also Charles R. Anderson, *Emily Dickinson's Poetry* (1960) 300–307.

The tension that is felt when five is counterpointed against four beats is greatly increased in the poem by tensions that operate within the four-beat lines. Regular tetrameter would have eased those tensions, and lessened the sense of perilous balance.

VIII

The motion picture *Tom Jones* is historically wrong but emotionally right to set the scene in church to Watts's Psalm 90, and use the tune St Anne as a bridge into Fielding's parody of Homeric struggle in the church yard. Squire Weston's church could not have sung Watts then nor even a century later, but the epic mood is right.

> Sufficient is Thine arm alone,
> And our defense is sure.

Here is one of her hymns to the unalterable Infinite. (350)

> They leave us with the Infinite.
> But He — is not a man —
> His fingers are the size of fists —
> His fists, the size of men —

Watts's clear anthropomorphic vision is sliding out of focus. His cosmic view fragments in the chaos of experienced fear. Hands and feet and fingers and fists and arms waver in surrealistic irrelevance. And the Rock of Ages moves about so, from one continent to another.

> And whom He foundeth, with his Arm
> As Himmaleh shall stand —
> Gibralter's Everlasting Shoe
> Poised lightly on his Hand.

Queasy from the first, the poet pulls herself together with commendable courage for a fine brisk close.

> So trust him, Comrade —
> You for you, and I, for you and me
> Eternity is ample,
> And quick enough, if true.

I do not postulate a mathematical equation between slant of truth and slant of rhyme, but I do think so conscious an artist could have thought of changing "you and me" to "me and you" if she had wanted true rhyme on that final chord. Rhyme and grammar lapse together into the conditional mode.

Her trust was in the Unexpected, her defense was to remind herself how ludicrous we are when we fancy the ways of the Infinite are predictable in nice easy common measure.

She prepares us for something like Psalm 121, in common measure (766) with rhyme words from hymns (decay-way, hill-will, arise-Paradise), but frustrates the reader by calculated shock tactics when the final rhyme goes off key in a most unhymnic figure of speech. The abrupt slanting of the rhyme is part and parcel of the tactics. Look to the hills? Let the hills look to me, "The Rivet in the Bands." The hymn closes with an effect like that of the *Tierce de Picardie*, which revolves a minor tune on a final major chord, jumping from "sharp key" to "flat key" for a resolution. In American and English hymnody, the Picardy third is unorthodox. It suddenly thrusts the hymn into an exotic musical convention. Modern composers and arrangers use it for shock effect, to startle and provoke thought by means of the unexpected.

Watts's grandest hymn, the grandest of English hymns, closes on the theme of the dedication of all to God.

> Were the whole realm of nature mine
> That were a present far too small;
> Love so amazing, so divine
> Demands my soul, my life, my all. (c, 7)

Emily Dickinson never forgot the stanza.[32] The rhyme words appear in natural association with the idea of "All is the price of all," whether human or heavenly magnificence. She never made a dedication to heavenly majesty, though she often contemplated its demand. She might beg to be excused in polite words and haunting melody (1024). Or she might perform a *cadenza d'inganno* on the theme.

> And then — the size of this "small" life —
> The Sages — call it small —
> Swelled — like Horizons — in my breast —
> And I sneered — softly — "small"! (271)

Identical rhyme is a violation of convention that sneers with the verb.

Rhetoric could flat the final chord. A characteristic method was to make some ringing statement of truth, then follow it with an anticlimactic clause that placed the whole truth at second hand: "So the Sages say," "So the

---

[32] *Letters* II 593 actually alludes to this Watts hymn in affectionate tone, but she had forgotten Watts wrote it.

Strong believe," "It is said." Or she queried the truth: "If true," "If heaven indeed redeem," "If God hear, that is," "If Jesus was sincere." The voicing is comic in effect, and marvellously true to regional speech patterns, refusing responsibility for grandiloquence and dropping pitch to undercut it in un-inflected tones. But she could make the construction carry all the bitterness of her unbelief when it came upon her, all her resentment of sages who had offered her truth that was not true for her.

Watts told her how a saint dies. She had known the hymn from childhood, but it may have struck with increased force when she had to sing it imme-diately after announcement was made of the death of a classmate.[33]

> Jesus can make a dying bed
> Feel soft as downy pillows are
> As on His breast we lay our head
> And breathe our life out gently there.
>
> O, if my Lord would come and meet,
> My soul would stretch its wings in haste — (b, 31)

All her life she sought verification of that glorious leave-taking. She wanted to know every detail of the last moments of friends. In the normal course of a woman's duty she was with the dying and the dead. Only in the past few years, and even now only in restricted areas, has the American Way of Death so divided life from death. It was from life, and from death, that she painted her superb pietas of New England deathbeds. She saw the convulsions, the beading of death-sweat, the veins "like Crayons," the jaw and hand frozen in agony, the glimmer of dead eyes between half-closed lids. But the King (465) did not come into the room, unless Death be Lord. The only wings were those of a fly buzzing.

There is scandalous frivolity in her hymns on the Last Judgment. In hymns, certain rhyme words occur in pairs so often that the matching amounts almost to a cliché. Three times in one lyric (409) she tempts the reader to anticipate the rhyme word *grace*, but grace is not pronounced at this Vision of Judgment. One parody of both hymn and sermon (234) begins with the text (Matthew 7:13–14) and moves quickly, as sermons were liable to do, from the strait gate to the bourse. Nineteenth-century preachers were adept at converting metaphysical ideas to dollars and cents. The poem is a check-list of possibilities about the soul's destiny. She checks it lackadaisi-cally up to the point where logic demands that she subscribe to a belief in

[33] Leyda I 145–146.

hell. The rhyme word to be matched is *Dividend*, and one supposes that its mate should properly have been *end*. But it is the poem that ends. It breaks off short in mid-line. No rhyme. No meter. No comment. A finished poem, not an unfinished one, closes in that abrupt silence.

Watts Entire ends with hymns for the Lord's supper. Emily Dickinson never joined the church and did not receive the sacrament, but many times at the table from which she was excluded, she heard:

> 'Tis Living Bread! We thank thee, Lord.
> We thank thee, Lord. 'Tis generous wine.   (c, 18)

Watts's adjective *generous* is at once obvious and simple, and precise to the point of subtlety in both the common and the etymological meanings. She searched her lexicon to contradict it. She was able to associate the idea of hospitality with the invitation given to the dying thief on the cross (1180, 1305), but she could not understand the sacrament. She always said so, and it seems important to believe her; her use of imagery in all her poetry indicates that she told the truth. The bee has generous wine. The sacrament of summer days is indeed lavish. But the "Bread of Heaven resents bestowal/ Like an obloquy" (1314). The table was meager, scanty, economical, inhospitable. The breaking of the bread reminded her of the feeding of birds (690, 773, 791), and the crumb that would have sufficed her smallness was not given. Her most horrendous statement on the subject uses no obviously religious vocabulary (941). A string of Watts's characteristic terms and attitudes chills the blood by its unstated analogy. A woman slowly starves a pet bird. Arbitrary and self-sufficient deity withholds the saving crumb from a helpless and adoring worshiper.

Bunyan wrote the Puritan epic of the Holy War as a spiritual conflict. Milton, after his ideals for England were defeated, wrote his epic about Man. *Watts Entire* externalized the War, assigning names and dates to the victories of God's people. Born the year Milton died, suckled in prison when his mother visited his father who was repeatedly jailed for his religious beliefs, Watts lived until 1748, his life spanning the years when Dissent became a recognized part of the social structure.[34] His songs are imbued with a sense of history moving under God's hand. Editors in America altered a few details of names and dates after the Revolutionary War, but the interpretation of history was intensified once they were sure who God's people really were.

---

[34] Bernard Lord Manning, *The Hymns of Wesley and Watts* (1962), p 78. V. De Sola Pinto, "Isaac Watts and the Adventurous Muse," *Essays and Studies of the English Association* (1935), 86–87. Both writers discuss the effect of historical circumstance on Watts's writing.

After the Revolution, the American fuguing tune became very popular. The tunes, Windham, China, Lisbon, Coronation, are in Emily Dickinson's earliest hymnbook. To such tunes the "Strong Hallelujahs roll." Sing Perronet's "All hail the power of Jesu's name" slowly and soberly to Dundee, and you have psalm style. Then recall how the words sounded on Christmas recordings by professional singers, and you have the finest of American fuguing tunes, Coronation by Oliver Holden. Sing Dundee again, this time using Watts's Psalm 98. Then remember how the carolers sang and almost danced it to Antioch, Lowell Mason's most vivacious style, "Joy to the world."

With this style Mason drove out the fuguing tunes, which became in the controversy a rallying point of True Blue Americanism in its losing fight against Mason's foreign imports — for Antioch is made from *Messiah*, and his tune Hamburg to which we sing Watts's "When I survey the wondrous cross" is made from a Gregorian chant. Modern hymnbooks use Coronation, but fill in the silent parts, obscuring the delayed entrances necessary for fuguing. Professional singers restore its pristine democratic verve, and, perfectly sung, Coronation is a harmony of freedoms, happily receiving individual styles without diminishing individuality. I have heard the very different styles of Jerome Hines, George Shea, and Ethel Waters stand clear and clean as they led 18,000 voices, hundreds of them professional singers, thousands of them choir trained, in Coronation. As if auditioning for the song around the Great White Throne, exultant individuality praised Omnipotence and no voice was lost.

The Masonites in the heat of controversy wrote descriptions of performances that persuade one that democracy can result in excruciating cacaphony. Writing from the other faction reminds one by its impassioned rhetoric that some people are not happy to relegate either their democracy or their counterpoint to professionals even for the sake of a more polished performance. Anthony Trollope could have told the tale. In *Barchester Towers* he framed his plot on the lively question of the Oxford Movement: What and how shall we sing in church? He knew the vast issues that hang on the choir loft and knew their genre was comedy.

Emily Dickinson rarely tried to record the sound of any voice other than her own, but one poem (426) vaguely suggests the fuguing tune. Frazar Stearnes, son of the president of Amherst College, was killed in action in a Union victory in North Carolina. Mr Dickinson, curt in his grief, blurted out the news, and for a long time Austin could not quit repeating his father's words. The poem describing the incident is not a success. Its tattered tetrameters show no force nor control. The voices are not clearly distinguished.

A third, and perhaps a fourth voice offer advice, not in universal truth but
in terms of evasion of truth. Whereas idealism once had spoken of martyrdom, the voices can find no better word than murder. The dry tones, exaggerated colloquialism, images of altering and saving of garments, attempt
to portray a community of sorrow undergirded by those Puritan virtues that
sometimes survive Puritan faith — thrift, restraint, family solidarity.

Her best refutation of Watts on the Holy War was silence. Amherst's Holy
War is absent from her pages. She did not even mention the songs sung by
both sides that now are background music for motion pictures about the
Civil War. Those nearest her ignored the war as best they could. Her brother
bought his way out. The man she may have loved and surely idealized,
Charles Wadsworth, announced from his pulpit that the Trojan War would
not take place. When it did, he went to California. His going may have
bewildered her whether she was in love with him or not. He had been singing Watts for years. Frazar Stearnes was buried on March 22 1862. On
April 15 she wrote her first letter asking help of a stranger. Higginson's critical acumen has been questioned, but not his role in the war.

Her poetry has teased many readers into supplying what the poetry does
not give, a coherent explanation of her life and the reader's. While it seems
a bit absentminded of some critics to overlook patent facts as they do (such
as: there was a war on, she never mentioned it, lyric poets may suffer from
enforced silence, silence may have been enforced by her most obvious trait,
loyalty), it is the quality of the poetry that concerns me, not the poet's
secrets, if any. The poetry excites, but does not satisfy. It is a poetry of
sensation, of ecstasy, of hunger, of pain — and it assigns no significance to
the pain it feels. There is no coherent vision of life, but rather a thousand
vignettes, clear, intensely seen, beautiful, telling all the truth she had to
offer. This poor lone poem should have been a masterpiece, standing in her
poetry as "Easter 1916" stands in the poetry of Yeats. Poor and lone as it is,
the poem tells all the truth she had to offer on this subject, and gives all the
advice she had for her brother: "Translate pain into another language. It
won't shriek so." That is what she did.

The central idea of Watts's *Logic* is that earth is propadeutic to heaven.
Watts was Mr Wadsworth's favorite poet, and one of his favorite metaphors
was "God's kindergarten." [35] The image scintillates through Emily Dickinson's early poetry in many moods.

---

[35] Mary Elizabeth Barbot, "Emily Dickinson Parallels," *New England Quarterly* xiv (December 1941), 689–696, develops the statement in Whicher (p 111) of a relationship between
Wadsworth's sermons and Emily Dickinson's poetry.

> I shall know why — when Time is over —
> And I have ceased to wonder why —
> Christ will explain each separate anguish
> In the fair schoolroom of the sky —
>
> He will tell me what "Peter" promised —
> And I — for wonder at his woe —
> I shall forget the drop of Anguish
> That scalds me now — that scalds me now.   (193)

The poem has been much admired. I agree with those who offer it as proof of poetic genius and religious conviction, but on my own terms. The second stanza, where the caesurae shift to try out the Robert Burns trick she was then using, is not very good, but the first stanza is quite perfect. It has a romantic tune we recognize as Heber's sweet voice, "Bread of the world in mercy broken." She also knew it, but knew many well-forgotten hymns to this tune by female hymnodists. That stanza sounds to me like a total parody of all hymns written by nineteenth-century females. It is silly. A *De Profundis* from the depths of exhaustion and the silliness that comes with it.

To explode a genre, a writer must work from within with knowledge of all its breastworks. That stanza jolts the mind from lyric mood to critical evaluation of statements commonly associated with the form. The jolt is greater because the sound is so lovely — quite as lovely as the sound of Mr Eliot's Hippotamus being kissed by all the martyred virgins. Almost ready to concede from weariness, sound and shape are the concessive devices. They say unanswerably, "Yes. I know all you can say on this subject, know it better than you do, for if you did, you could write like this. A thousand times I have heard: 'THEN God will make His justice known.' By then I won't care. I don't think I care much now."

Still, as a master hymnodist, she could sound the exquisite flagging notes, and raise the one theological question no one has answered. Like "The Hippotamus" it is a religious poem, unorthodox in method, filing faint protest in that second line against a cheap and easy notion of perfect love and omniscience. Neither it nor "The Hippotamus" would make good hymns, but they give people who sing hymns something to think about. Not palinodes, erasing all the Church has said, but parodies, rousing minds lulled by reiteration of expected sounds. The poets' panurgy gives credential. These are not outsiders speaking. They have a vote.

I X

An encounter between Little Emily and Dr Watts:

> "Arcturus" is his other name —
> I'd rather call him "Star."
> It's very mean of science
> To go and interfere!
>
> I slew a worm the other day —
> A "Savant" passing by
> Murmured "Resurgam" — "Centipede"!
> "Oh Lord — how frail are we"!   (70)

"I shall arise." Watts's most characteristic gesture was flying off to heaven.[36] "Call the thing by its correct scientific name." "Meditate on it as emblem of man's shortcomings."

Samuel Johnson said of Watts, "He has provided instruction for all ages, from those who are lisping their first lessons to the enlightened readers of Malebranche and Locke; he has left neither corporeal nor spiritual nature unexamined; he has taught the Art of Reasoning and the Science of the Stars." [37]

Legend gave Watts knowledge of Latin at four, Greek at six, Hebrew at seven years of age.[38] The brilliant boy was offered opportunity to go to Oxford, but rather than conform to the Church of England, he chose to attend schools set up by Dissenters. He lost the high patina Oxford can put on classical studies, but gained the approval of conscience, the wider curriculum of the Dissenting schools, and a completely happy experience with educational processes. His experience as teacher was as happy as his own schooling. He never thought of himself as unusual, and conferred his own precocity on all children and his love of learning on all mankind, thinking the acquisition and imparting of knowledge was man's natural joy at any age. He wrote very successful textbooks on science and philosophy, very influential treatises on education, and a *Logic* that was standard at both universities through the century and in wide use for a hundred and fifty years. Sage, Savant, Scientist, he was also authority on child-rearing and hero of the faith.

---

[36] The worm, however, will not arise. The human body was resurrectible, but "Worms and Moles" were to be destroyed in the general conflagration. Emily Dickinson, on the other hand, insisted on a heaven for daisies and rats, said she would not go to heaven if it had no place for blue jays, and certainly envisioned a winged eternity for worms.

[37] Samuel Johnson, *The Lives of the Poets*, 2 vols (1946) II 298.

[38] Actually, Latin at five, Greek at eight, French at ten, Hebrew at thirteen years of age.

He blended Calvinism, Milton's Christian humanism, and Locke's empiricism into something I shall call a doctrine of reason as a means of grace. Reason lost its native place when Adam fell. Unassisted, it could not guide man, perceive God's glory nor discern God's will. Faith was needed, arbitrary gift of God. But Watts denied the positions of both Calvin and Locke by his insistence on an innate moral sense, "a sort of pathetick instinct or disposition toward goodness." The mind and the soul were synonymous, he said, and he pictured Reason as a winged thing.

Means of grace, from a human point of view, are channels by which God gives preventing, sanctifying, or justifying grace; theological positions are defined with reference to the doctrine of grace.[39] In describing this process of transfer from God to man, Watts elevated the part played by human volition (man's will to know and do God's will) and by human reason. Reason, being man's highest attribute simply as man, must stretch its wings in constant effort toward that upward flight. Though Reason's highest flight, compared to the Most High, would seem "groveling," no failure was final, and in its flight it gave off the angels' song of "Glory to God." It sang also of "Peace on earth." Watts said he learned religious toleration from Locke, the "wondrous man" so mightily used of God in His work of Enlightenment. Watts postulated the possibility of successive stages in the hallowing of the mental processes. To this end, the study of logic must be pursued with confidence and vigor. The pursuit was no passive acceptance of a divine gift. Will, energies, reason were involved. His hymns reflect his beliefs, both in logical structure and in specific conclusions from his learned disputations, such as the resurrectibility of the body and the nature of absolute space. He felt himself responsible for not falsifying any truth as he saw it. For the singers of his hymns, of whatever intellectual attainments, he claimed the domain of higher intellection by planting there, as firmly as he could, the banner of the Cross.

---

[39] The controversial points were the parts played by volition, reason, and deeds of charitable intent; the theologians most prominently involved in controversy were agreed that "with regard to God, there is no such thing as means," for God works by any means or none. The alleged antinomianism of the "enthusiasts" was a crux. When controversy arose between Whitefield and Bishop Secker, Watts refused to comment, although it seems that his whole argument was relevant. See Thomas Wright, *The Life of Watts* (1914) 203–204. Wright, an admiring biographer, speaks at this point of Watts's "mischievous amiability . . . his quixotic desire to minimize the difference between Christians." But Watts's position was based on this "mischievous amiability." It is almost impossible to exaggerate the degree to which he was accepted by all parties as absolutely central to the theology of the period. Later, however, when the Augustan thinking became suspect, Watts came under question. Samuel Johnson found him orthodox; Robert Southey was by no means certain that he was.

Emily Dickinson was not a systematic philosopher, but in fairness to her constant objection to this system of thought, it may be noted that others have found it unsatisfactory. It has been attacked both as an arrogation of the intellect and as an abandonment of it. Quietists have thought it busy and bustling; revolutionary spirits of the latter part of the eighteenth century thought it too quietly content with the *status quo*. Sir Leslie Stephens called it "a crude amalgam." [40] Passionate and devout intellectuals have said that the Augustan eirenicon was a compromise seeking peace at any price — passion, faith, intellect. If it seem a placebo, its very mildness commended it to men who thought the bitter remedies of an earlier day had not worked very well, who hoped in a new concept of the universal correspondences of universal law, who hoped that enlightened men would discern the correspondences and live reasonably in accord with them of their own will. It seemed that Newton and Locke had predicted it.

Upon her return from seminary, Emily Dickinson assumed, partly in jest, an anti-intellectual stance that preceded and hardened into her rejection of formal religion, which in Amherst was almost co-extensive with formal education. Watts was the very type of pious and precocious youth. There is little evidence of the kind of child she was, but in her mature writing she chose to represent herself as one unbelievably maledroit in linguistic matters, repeatedly ascribing literal meaning to some symbol. Any family can match a few such yarns as her confusing *atom* with Adam, or amputation with "Is the Lord's hand waxed short?" Her misapprehensions multiply into a *Book of Boners* that seems to be fiction modeled on Watts's examples of sophism, *ignoratio elenchi* and *non causa pro causa*. Her failure to grasp the basic plot of Bible stories, her plodding density of interpretation, would put her out of court if her purpose were theological disputation. Except in a special sense, that is not her purpose. She constantly protests the danger of one sort of inference, of giving a child a major premise couched as a proverb or intrinsic in some symbol from which premise he is to reason by analogy. When experience proves the premise false, the child is forced to "infer" that all men are swindlers.

Watts's *Logic* was admittedly weakest in its treatment of direct inference. His unwilling pupil made up for the lack. She reasons by inference, a logical process in which "certain things being stated, something other than what is stated follows of necessity from their being so." From 1862 on, the word

[40] Leslie Stephens, *English Thought in the Eighteenth Century*, 2 vols (1902) II 386.

infer is prominent in her writing.[41] The only data admitted as valid are received directly from experience, and interpreted by the imagination. Validity being thus restricted, her thought is inferential and her conception is imagistic. Conclusions vary because experience varies. Images vary in meaning because everything they image may fluctuate.

The figures of speech in her poetry are so affected by this mode of thought that she stands as the Puritan iconoclast *par excellence,* or at least *in extremis.* She had no sacred images. Any figure of speech might carry any degree of solemnity. Not one carries a stable content of emotion or idea. If tropes be reduced to mathematical equations, with one half simply equal to the other, the similarity between her and Watts is great, the same images occurring most frequently in both bodies of verse, and appearing in the same arbitrary associations. The poetic use made of the tropes throughout her work is very different. She made jokes about being "Betrothed to Righteousness." She often identified herself in sympathy with the white-clad martyr throng and the characters in Foxe's *Book of Martyrs,* but she joked about "the fires of Smithfield," spoke of the cup of martyrdom as a patent medicine endorsed by Stephen, and alluded to the Seven Last Words as the cries of an auctioneer.

She wrote riddle poems, but no emblem poems save such as her take-off on Watts's worm (885), where "It's all sing-song in the Watts countree," and in jest she established Watts's famous moral formula, worm:man::man: God.[42]

Like the metaphysical wits, and unlike Samuel Johnson, she thought God enjoyed jokes, but the likeness ends there. Her jokes were different. There is little evidence of her reading of these poets, but if she had known them by heart (as Watts almost did), she would not have used conceits; nor did Watts use conceits in his hymns, though he did use baroque conceits in *Horae Lyricae,* and used the seventeenth-century poetry as a treasure trove for his hymns, where the figures of speech are simplified and reduced to a density he thought appropriate for use in hymns. Every "metaphysical conceit" that has been discovered in her poetry is in Watts, but in neither her poetry nor his does it remain a conceit. A genuine conceit wrenches the two parts of the trope into a new intellectual relationship; it is born of wit and

[41] The word (476, 564, 797, 823, 843, 856, 951, 1163, 1258, 1279, 1411, 1467, 1471, 1646) can be compared to *guess, surmise, intimate* (576, 726, 1187, 1195, 1608, 1632, 1702), and with such a wish as some poems express (954) to be able to reason from known chemical laws to the unknown. It seems that the product of her inference is a truth, in a sense that is not true of these other mental processes.

[42] She would not accept this formula under any circumstances; see *Letters* II 339, where her beloved Dr Dwight offered it to her as a metaphor. Riddle poems: 140, 221, 228, 311, 391, 517, 884, 1114, 1337, 1397, 1463, 1468, 1669, etc.

perceived by wit; it demonstrates radical congruence, some likeness at the root of the trope. Her quasi-conceits are born of humor and demonstrate radical incongruity.

By her reckoning, any real definition (as opposed to a nominal definition) must be made from experience and stated as image. Her many definitions of abstract terms are thus constructed. Trained in methodical definition, writing as one who made her lexicon her companion, she played with *definiens* and *definiendum* to disprove the over-simple equivalences of savants who handled words as if they had fixed numerical values.

From the disciplines of formal education she contrived subtle images, and used them to prove that nothing of significance was to be learned from optics, chemistry, philology, comparative anatomy, logic, grammar, mathematics, and entomology. Her father was lawyer, politician, treasurer to Amherst College; she used spontaneously and correctly the vocabulary of his daily occupations. Watts also used the vocabulary in such a manner that one can identify his hymns by its presence, or bracket one's shots when guessing at authorship of an unknown hymn. His business-like assessments ("When I survey . . . , My richest gain I count but loss") and his legal transactions ("When I can read my title clear") do not imply that in this best of all possible worlds the ledgers and statute books of men correlate perfectly with eternal Gain and universal Law. But they do imply, and he did believe, that man while yet in time could discern that law and assess that gain. He looked to an hour when his title should be declared legal, would "speak," as a document is said to speak, from the hour when it becomes part of the corpus of the law. Her "Title Divine" had validity only in her imagination.

The hymns, and the English and Latin poems of Watts typically end with a powerful upward surge, an image of flight bringing with it certain associations. His space-flights are almost Miltonic in grandeur. Milton delegated the flying to spirits, but Watts did his own. The Abyss held no terrors for him. Outer space was his playground. He longed for "pinions of my own." He felt himself "an exile of the sky." "Heaven is my element," he said, "and I must use my wings."

This image was in no way "sacred" in Emily Dickinson's poetry. She felt with intense kinesthesia the flight of birds and few have equalled the accuracy and élan with which she transmits it. She knew such people as Watts existed; she spoke of them (262) and identified one by name — Charles Wadsworth was "an Aborigine of the sky." [43] She could feel by a sort of

---

[43] *Letters* III 901.

spiritual kinesthesia in the "Sinews from within" a response to the great *sursum corda* of death when it came to them. She herself was no such person. The idea of moving through space evoked sensations of nausea and vertigo, of being lost where great streets of silence open out on No Universe, of reeling down something like an interminable hotel corridor, where, even if "Knock and it shall be opened" were a promise to trust, she was unable to "infer" God's address. This lost estate is not symbolic so much as symptomatic, accurate clinical record of the effect of shock.

She was in love with Judge Lord and he loved her. After his death, she stood before his portrait and answered the "ascension" in the pictured face:

> Go thy great way!
> The Stars thou meetst
> Are even as Thyself —
> For what are Stars but Asterisks
> To point a human Life? [44]

She would have her pun on punctuation, but puns have been made sacred by other poets. Her pun on punctuation (asterisk = star + punctuation mark) would perhaps have passed muster in serious poetry of the early seventeenth century, but at this date it was not a "sacred" rhetorical device. In another sense, the poem was not sacred to this occasion, but sacred to the sensation she records. When the sensation came again, she sent the poem to a friend applying it to a quite different situation. The poem is not about Judge Lord, but about how she felt at that moment.

Watts's famous quatrain could stand as epigraph to some of her best poetry:

> The tulip and the butterfly
> Appear in gayer coats than I;
> Let me be drest fine as I will,
> Flies, worms and flowers exceed me still.   (Song 22)

The *sententia* on the vanity of human wishes is, of course, missing from her poems. So is the generalization of the word *coats*, which blurs the niceties of observation. Augustan poets, as we know, did not speak in detail about tulips and their streaks. She clothed the small creatures of her garden in *haut couture*, her accuracy of observation matched by her knowledge of vogue. Each frill, tassel, bead, parasol, surcingle, hat brim, veil, ruffle and fringe is in place. In this day of ready-made, drip-dry planned obsolescence,

---

[44] On Judge Lord's portrait, *Letters* III 860, and poem no. 1638. The same poem to Mrs James S. Cooper, *Letters* III 863.

her poetry reminds us of the time once spent in construction and care of garments. All details of her seamstress-science — even the difficulty of sweeping a room where dressmaking has taken place — are used in her poetry with penurious economy. She used with finesse the metaphysical overtones of fabrics. Gauze differs in essence from brocade, dimity from broadcloth.[45] She was not unaware of a basic symbolism of garments; she knew that brides wear white and empresses wear purple, and some of her "tragic" uses of the ideas are moving. None moves me, however, like the comic poems using this figure of speech written during the years 1862 to 1864. The most frequent image in all her poetry is that of clothing. The sensation recorded is anxiety lest she not be properly dressed. That is trite enough. Civilization will totter when women are not interested. In the direst circumstances, women are made to understand that it is sulking to refuse to be interested. By her very concern, she persuades me that civilization has tottered. The world is shaken and chaos is come again.

It insults uniqueness to read her as Emerson-and-water or Donne *manqué*. As man and as poet, Donne had resources not open to her, and Emerson could draw a moral from the fresh rhodora in the wood. Not she. Her acts are not sacramental, the garments are not symbolic. Nothing she makes, mends, or wears will have significance beyond itself. But she had resources, not the least of which was genuine good humor.

She fends off all generalities; the *Old Farmer's Almanac*, Bartlett's *Familiar Quotations*, Watts on the Song of Solomon do not apply. Ophelia's "Oh, you must wear your rue with a difference" is an excellent fashion hint when spoken to a tragedy queen, but in Amherst mourning was conventional. Emily Dickinson observed the fashions of the Cross as if she watched the fall showings, lest her sorrow appear *outré*, hardly hoping for even this surface and social correspondence, for she had no right to her mourning.

One may be many things in absolute loneliness, but not fashionable. She stages her tragedy by her very acceptance of those social principles without which comedy cannot exist. It is the final absurdity, the absolute of loneliness, to postulate vogue *in vacuo*. One who does not care to look at anything so quiveringly alive can easily congeal her into an emblem of patience on a monument, a complex, a symbol of faith, hope, and charity. But in fact there is no abstraction to shield her from the point of that needle.

---

[45] Gauze, brocade, dimity, broadcloth, damask, chintz, muslin, fustian, plush, organdy, satin, silk, velvet, tartan, lace, cashmere, mechlin, sackcloth, tulle, cambric, tapestry. She speaks of hat making, patchwork, ripped seams, seamless knitting, alterations, "piecing." She used the word *stitch* to designate the final closing, as opposed to basting, which is temporary.

Her figures of speech that image God are all in Watts or given pretext by Watts,[46] but the theological sum is different. Watts added as he saw fit to Calvinism. She subtracted the belief in hell; with it goes all that is serious in Calvinism, but not all that is confusing in life. She knew her own stubbornness, and knew better than Watts that it was God's nature to be arbitrary. She was quite dependable, but God's terrible fickleness was manifest. Her time was correct. God might be punctual, or might snort in late in a flurry of whirlwind, or might be rudely too early, making Himself known by His intrusions. There was no relying on His "duplicity." She held herself up as a good example, and, just in case He might be capable of logic, set Him elementary problems in her own brand of inference. From His experiences as man, He should be able to infer her pain. From His experiences with saints and martyrs, He could infer how good she would have been had He seen fit to give her faith. If the conclusion of the syllogism was only imaginary goodness, what could He expect? The Elect have faith. The Strong mount on wings of reason. Only the image-making faculty with which she was endowed could stretch for her a taut line between world and world. And, as they said in Amherst and Mt Holyoke, she "entertained hope." Her last poem that is phrased as a prayer expresses a hope that God might manage to be changeless (1689).

"You ask my Books," she wrote to Higginson. "For Poets I have. . . ." Dr Watts? Never. But he was there. Contending against "the Thews of Hymn," she developed some Sinews from within to keep her nimbleness from being limp and lush and unmuscled.[47]

---

[46] By giving pretext, I mean such a phrase as "Holy Ghosts in cages." Watts never watched the circus unload, but his realistic and memorable Lion of Judah (b, 53) and Psalm 58 gave her pretext. The circus added the cage. Watts did not picture God as a sly and dishonest businessman; but his Psalm 78 gives pretext if one so choose to interpret the awful irony of answered prayer. Watts did not write the Song of Solomon, but he gave to a church that had been pining to sing its own love song since 1549 two excellent usable song cycles on the book. These were greatly loved in New England, and even when love had cooled, they were given to the young as being safer than the original, as well as doctrinally sound and memorable.

[47] *Letters* II 404. The poem quoted is 616.

Poem 350 and lines from other poems are reprinted by permission of the publishers and the Trustees of Amherst College from Thomas H. Johnson, Editor, *The Poems of Emily Dickinson*, Cambridge, Mass: The Belknap Press of Harvard University Press, Copyright 1955, by The President and Fellows of Harvard College. Lines from poems 597 and 766 are quoted from *The Complete Poems of Emily Dickinson* edited by Thomas H. Johnson, by permission of Little, Brown and Company. Lines from poems 1522 and 1545 are quoted from *Life and Letters of Emily Dickinson*, edited by Martha Dickinson Bianchi, by permission of Houghton Mifflin Company.

Extended Notes

Note for page 40:

[20] I cannot identify the source of this psalm, nor of Psalm CIV, no. 5 section III. The copy of Osborn's reprint in the Union Theological Seminary Library has a penciled note: "J. Broughton?" Luke Tyerman, *Life of John Wesley*, 3 vols (London 1870) I 67, 103, and elsewhere, identifies Broughton as J. Broughton; but in his later study, *The Oxford Methodists* (1873) 334–360, Tyerman gives a detailed biography of him as Thomas Broughton. Broughton has been confused with John Broughton, the psychologist, whose *Psychologia* (1704) was part of the deist controversy, his chief opponent being William Coward, *The Grand Essay* (1704). He has also been confused with Thomas Broughton, vicar of St Mary Redcliffe in Bristol and author of Handel's libretto for *Hercules*. But Broughton was neither, nor was he that more famous John Broughton, the father of British pugilism. He was a member of Exeter College, Oxford, one of the very early members of the group of Oxford Methodists; he once gave John Wesley some verses, of which no record remains unless this conjecture be correct. See *DNB* and index of standard editions of John Wesley's sermons, journals, and letters.

Note for page 54:

[16a] Professor G. E. Bentley, Jr, upon reading this statement in the *Bulletin*, generously wrote to offer a qualification of my certitude. There is a possibility, he says, that *Songs of Experience* may have been issued separately by Blake. — M.W.E.

The case is that we know of 21 solitary copies of *Innocence*, 24 copies of the combined *Innocence* and *Experience*, and only 2 solitary copies of *Experience* — each having folio numbering that implies a now lacking preceding copy of *Innocence*. (There are two fragmentary selections of plates from *Experience*, about which little can be deduced.) Some of the combined sets, however, have separate foliation for each group (some have no numbering); it is not unlikely that some copies of *Experience* were printed, colored, and bound separately — but apparently only to supply persons who already possessed copies of *Innocence*. — D.V.E.

Index